The HUNGRY STUDENT
Cookbook

The HUNGRY STUDENT *Cookbook*

Charlotte Pike

CONTENTS

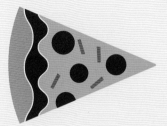

INTRODUCTION

Feeding yourself at uni can be a real challenge. And doing it on a budget can make eating good food downright difficult, never mind cramped kitchens, limited equipment and cookers with a mind of their own. Welcome to student life!

But you don't have to resort to endless takeaways and baked beans, tempting as that may be. With this book and a few key kitchen tools, you can eat great food on a budget every day, whatever the state of your kitchen. Result. Even if you're a complete beginner with no clue where to start, this book will show you how. And if you're already a keen cook and want to show off to your friends, you'll find plenty of inspiration too. Whatever your level, you'll discover budget-friendly ideas, yummy food and loads of useful tips. Time to get cooking!

There are many reasons why cooking your own food from scratch is a great idea. For a start, it can be far quicker and cheaper than buying microwave meals or takeaways, saving you money for other things. It also ensures you know exactly what's in your food – no nasty surprises in your ready meal! And a tight budget doesn't have to mean dreary, bland dinners. The recipes in this book have all passed the taste test! You may need to stock up on a few spices and seasonings, but a little of these goes a long way. And remember that you can cook large batches to last you for a couple of days, or freeze the excess in separate portions to pull out when you're too busy (or skint) to do a big shop or spend time cooking.

Making the effort to prepare a good meal that fits around your timetable (and your social life) can be great fun and even stress-busting. When in a black hole of revision, there's nothing like taking some time away from the laptop to tinker in the kitchen. Or crank up some music and cook for your friends – they might even help you wash the dishes...! All of the recipes in this book can be made easily in a humble student kitchen with minimal equipment. Whatever your skill level, you *can* cook delicious meals from scratch. This isn't just student food, it's great food!

USEFUL KITCHEN KIT

You don't need loads of fancy kitchen equipment to cook great food. Nor do you need everything ready for the first day of term; you can get by with just a few key items while you work out what else will be useful. See what you can share with housemates, too, particularly if you have a small kitchen with limited storage space.

Try to invest a little in any equipment you do buy. It's worth getting a solid frying pan, for example. Very cheap ones cook unevenly, resulting in burning or sticking, but a good one can last for many years. And it may sound like a luxury, but a blender or food processor will pay for itself with homemade dips, soups and smoothies. A stick blender is the most affordable type and comes with a variety of attachments for different jobs. For pricier items like these, see if your parents can help, or look out for bargains in the sales. Here are the main things you'll need:

Large non-stick frying pan or wok

Medium frying pan

Large and small saucepans, with lids

Ovenproof casserole dish with a lid

1.5-litre ovenproof baking dish (for puds)

Non-stick baking sheet

Large deep roasting tray

20cm square cake tin (for brownies, etc.)

Mixing bowl or large serving bowl

Microwavable/heatproof bowl (ideally glass)

Chopping board (white plastic is most hygienic)

Large and small sharp knives

Kitchen scissors

Wooden spoon(s)

Silicone spatula

Fish slice

Whisk

Can opener

Vegetable peeler

Garlic crusher (useful but not essential)

Potato masher (else just use a fork)

Pastry brush (useful but not essential)

Grater

Pepper grinder

Sieve

Colander

Measuring spoons

Measuring jug

Scales (electric are most accurate)

Rolling pin (or use a clean, dry wine bottle)

Wire cooling rack (or use a clean oven/grill shelf)

Oven gloves (or use a thick, folded tea towel)

Plastic boxes with lids

Thermos flask

LOVE YOUR OVEN

Every oven is different, so get to know yours. Some run hotter and others run cooler than the temperature they're set to. This doesn't have to be a problem, you just need to get used to it. Follow this advice to get the best from your oven:

* Most modern ovens are electric (with temperatures in degrees centigrade – generally 50–240°C). Look inside to see if yours has a fan at the back (these days, most do). If so, use the temperatures given throughout this book. If you have an electric oven without a fan, add 20°C to the stated cooking temperatures. And just in case you have a gas oven, the recipes also give temperatures in gas marks.

* Always preheat the oven well before you need to put your food in. Most have a thermostat light that comes on when you turn on the oven, and goes out when it reaches the correct temperature. Watch this the first time you use the oven and note how long it takes.

* Keep a close eye on cooking times. Where a recipe gives a range (e.g. 20–30 minutes), always check and test after the minimum (in this case 20 minutes) and, if required, return the food to the oven for some or all of the remaining time. This will ensure your cakes don't burn. It's worth bearing in mind that some ovens are just way out, and so recipes can take much, much longer than they are supposed to. It's useful to make a note next to the recipe of the actual time it ended up taking so you have the information handy for next time.

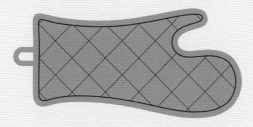

STOCKING UP YOUR STORE CUPBOARD

You can build up your collection of ingredients as you go along, or maybe ask your parents for a bit of help getting started. Some basics go a long way, so you could even club together with housemates and share. These items will see you through many recipes in this book:

Baking powder

Bicarbonate of soda

Butter (keep in the fridge)

Canned beans

Canned chickpeas

Canned sweetcorn

Canned tomatoes

Caster sugar

Cheese: Cheddar or similar, and Parmesan

Coconut milk

Concentrated tomato purée

Couscous

Flour: plain and self-raising

Frozen green vegetables

Garlic

Ginger

Herbs: thyme, rosemary, basil (fresh or dried)

Honey

Jam

Lemons and limes

Mayonnaise (keep in the fridge)

Milk (keep in the fridge)

Mustard

Noodles

Oats

Oils: sunflower/vegetable and olive oil

Olives (jars or cans are cheapest)

Onions

Pasta and spaghetti

Rice

Salt and pepper

Sauces: tomato, soy, sweet chilli

Spices: ground cinnamon, ground cumin, chilli powder, turmeric, fenugreek

Stock cubes: vegetable and chicken are the most versatile

Tuna (canned)

Yoghurt (plain or Greek is used in cooking)

WATCHING YOUR BUDGET

* **Eating out or buying packet sandwiches** can be a huge drain on your budget, so taking a packed lunch with you to campus, even if only occasionally, can save you a significant amount. Buying takeaway coffees can also be very expensive, so if you love coffee, invest in a cheap cafetière for making good coffee at home – it will soon pay for itself. A Thermos flask is handy for transporting your own tea, coffee or even soup instead of buying it on the go.

* **Before you go shopping, make a list** and plan carefully, based on what you have in the cupboard already and the meals you want to cook. Impulse buying can result in doubling up on items or forgetting a vital ingredient.

* **Shopping around makes a difference.** Be aware much you're paying for every item you buy, and check supermarket websites to see if another sells it more cheaply. Larger, out-of-town supermarkets tend to charge lower prices for many goods than smaller 'city' branches of the same chain. If you can't get to a large branch, then online shopping could be worthwhile – you get the benefit of those lower prices and can also buy some items in bulk (such as washing powder or toilet roll), which can save you cash in the long run. Why not club together with housemates to share the delivery charge?

* **Supermarkets aren't always the best place.** Some ethnic food items – including herbs, spices, rice, noodles, and sauces or flavoured pastes – can be more affordable from Asian or Caribbean grocery stores. And if you have a local market, it's often the cheapest place for fruit, veg, fresh herbs and sometimes even meat and fish (but beware farmers' markets, which sell mainly organic or premium products, at premium prices!).

* **For specialist items, look online.** Whole spices such as cinnamon sticks and vanilla pods tend to be very expensive on the high street, but can be found much cheaper from online suppliers.

* **Keeping it local can save you money** on fresh produce. There are a surprising number of local food cooperatives that sell affordable vegetable boxes. If you live in a city, many community allotments sell seasonal vegetables extremely cheaply, and sometimes even give them away. Often your local independent health food shop can put you in touch with these schemes, or you can search online. Some universities also operate vegetable box schemes, so do ask about this.

* **See if your parents will take you shopping** at the start of term. Stock up on herbs, spices, stock cubes, canned fish and beans, pasta, flour, sugar, etc. With a well-stocked store cupboard, you can pull together so many recipes in this book in a flash, without needing to buy too many extra ingredients.

* **Fresh herbs are a luxury but add a real edge** to home cooking. You could even grow your own on a windowsill – either buy living pots from the supermarket or grow some cuttings taken from the garden at home. Fresh basil, for example, will lift a simple tomato pasta dish and costs next to nothing if you keep a plant.

* **Buy a good-quality sunflower or vegetable oil** for everyday use – for roasting, baking, frying and greasing tins – but spend a little more on a decent bottle of olive oil (extra-virgin if you can stretch to it), for salad dressings and dips. Olive oil has a much nicer flavour, but works best cold.

HOW NOT TO POISON YOUR FRIENDS

Food hygiene might not sound rock-and-roll, but it's really important to get things right so you don't end up ill. Food poisoning is surprisingly common, so here's how to keep yourself and your friends safe.

HYGIENE

* When you first move into a house or halls, the kitchen may not be clean, so it's wise to clean all the surfaces, cupboards, sink and floor with antibacterial cleaner.

* Before touching any food, wash your hands well with hot water and soap. Wash them immediately after handling meat, and again after cooking.

* Keep on top of kitchen cleaning and don't let the dirty plates pile up. If you need to implement a cleaning rota with your housemates, then do it.

* Wipe up spillages and crumbs straight away, from work surfaces, inside the fridge and on the floor, using a separate mop or cloths for the floor.

* Keep the sink clean and throw away any bits that gather in the plughole every time you wash up.

* Wash up with hot, soapy water. Never wash up using cold water or without washing-up liquid.

* White plastic chopping boards are the cheapest and most hygienic and it's easy to see if they aren't clean. Keep a separate board for meat.

* Wash fabric cloths and tea towels regularly on a hot wash. Replace sponges or cloths regularly as they can be full of bacteria. If you drop a tea towel on the floor, put it straight in the wash.

* Sweep the floor often and take out the rubbish regularly. If there have been any spillages inside the bin, clean them as soon as you can, using hot water and washing-up liquid or an antibacterial cleaner. Remember that it's never worth economising on bin bags...

COOKING

* Ensure you prepare raw meat separately from any other ingredients and always wash your hands, board and knife really well in hot, soapy water immediately afterwards. This is particularly important when preparing raw chicken and turkey as they can carry salmonella.

* Make sure your food is properly cooked. Meat must be really hot, and when cooking chicken, turkey, pork, burgers and sausages, they should be cooked through entirely, with no pink meat in the centre and any juices running clear. Always cut open a piece to check. Steak and lamb can be served slightly pink in the centre and fish will flake once cooked.

* If you have leftovers, let them cool before wrapping and chilling in the fridge or freezing.

* Make sure food is thoroughly defrosted before reheating it. You can do this in the microwave on a defrost setting, or place the food on a plate, still in its wrapping, and leave at room temperature overnight.

* When reheating leftovers, make sure they are piping hot before serving. You may need to add 1–2 tablespoons of water to stop your food drying out whilst reheating. Only ever reheat food once - any more will mean the chances of harmful bacteria growing in your food increase.

SAFE STORAGE

* Any perishable foods, such as meat, fish and dairy products, should be kept in the fridge, sealed in their original packaging, with cling film or in a food bag. Put these items in the fridge as soon as you get home from shopping and return them to the fridge immediately after use.

* Store cooked and raw meat separately in the fridge and make sure they are well wrapped. Keep raw meat on the bottom shelf if you can, away from other produce. If this isn't possible, just make sure everything is well packaged.

* Don't have open packets or uncovered bowls of food in the fridge. Once you open a packet, seal it well, either by putting it in another bag and sealing with a knot or clip or by transferring it to a clean plastic container. Cover bowls of leftovers with cling film. Keep all packets in your cupboard sealed and store biscuits in an airtight box or tin. It will stop food going stale and prevent spillages or, worse, mice.

* Pay attention to use-by dates on food and try to use up everything before then. Discard any fresh ingredients that have been open for a few days.

* To store leftover canned food, always transfer it to a plastic tub with a lid. Never put open cans in the fridge, even if sealed, as they can release toxic chemicals into the food.

CLEVER COOKING

* It may sound obvious, but before you start cooking, check you have all the necessary ingredients and equipment – you don't want to have to rush out to the shops when you're halfway through a recipe!

* Read through the whole method before you begin, so you know exactly what you need to do and when. Allow plenty of time and don't be tempted to rush. Some recipes take time for a reason.

* If making a cake or pudding, remember that baking is the more scientific side of cooking. Measure all your ingredients accurately and use the specified tin sizes to ensure the recipe works as it should. Never open the oven door until the minimum cooking time has passed – your cake will turn out as flat as a pancake!

* If you're lacking equipment, be inventive. A clean wine or spirits bottle can be used to roll out pizza dough or pastry. If you don't have a blender, you can roughly mash ingredients with a potato masher or fork and a bit of elbow grease. If you don't have a colander, a sieve works just as well; and a clean oven or grill shelf does the same job as a cooling rack.

* Make the most of your freezer. If you freeze sliced bread, you'll always have some in for toast or quick lunches. Make large batches of casseroles or soups and freeze in separate bags, so you have a stash of instant meals-for-one. Stock up on frozen fruit and veg – they are great standby ingredients and often much cheaper than the fresh equivalents. Frozen berries are ideal for breakfast smoothies and baking, while frozen green beans, peas and spinach can be thrown into soups, stews and pasta bakes.

TOMATO AND GARLIC SPAGHETTI

Serves: 1 (Vegetarian)

Although this is probably one of the cheapest meals you can make, it definitely doesn't compromise on taste. It's also really easy to add other flavours to the sauce – see the suggested variation using anchovies, below.

100g dried spaghetti

1 tbsp olive oil

2 large garlic cloves, peeled

3 tbsp canned

chopped tomatoes

Salt and pepper

Parmesan (or vegetarian equivalent), finely grated, to serve (optional)

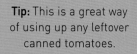

Tip: This is a great way of using up any leftover canned tomatoes.

* Boil the kettle and fill a large saucepan with the boiling water. Place on a medium heat and bring back up to the boil, then add a pinch of salt and the spaghetti. Cook for the time stated on the packet.

* Meanwhile, place the olive oil in a frying pan over a medium heat.

* Chop the garlic cloves finely and add to the frying pan, making sure it is not too hot – you don't want the garlic to colour, just to soften and release its flavour.

* Add the chopped tomatoes and allow to bubble away and thicken for 8 minutes or so – until the spaghetti in the other pan is cooked. Season the sauce to taste.

* Drain the spaghetti well in a colander, then return it to the saucepan. Pour in the tomato sauce and stir to combine.

* Serve immediately, topped with grated Parmesan, if you like.

TOMATO AND ANCHOVY SPAGHETTI
Follow the method above, but reduce the garlic to just one clove and increase the canned tomatoes to 4 tablespoons. When adding the tomatoes to the frying pan, also add two drained anchovies (from a can), chopped finely.

SPAGHETTI BOLOGNESE

Serves: 6

Bolognese is a classic pasta sauce that all first-time cooks should learn how to make. Although this recipe serves six, you can make the full quantity for yourself and keep leftovers well-wrapped in the fridge for 3 days, or divide into portions and freeze. For a speedy dinner, you can then defrost and reheat the sauce in the microwave for adding to cooked pasta.

2 tbsp olive oil

1 large onion, peeled and chopped finely

1 carrot, peeled and chopped into small cubes

2 garlic cloves, peeled and chopped finely

500g minced beef

2 rashers of bacon, chopped

4 tbsp tomato purée

150ml chicken stock

150ml red wine (optional)

2 x 400g cans chopped tomatoes

1 bay leaf

Salt and pepper

600g dried spaghetti

Parmesan, finely grated, to serve (optional)

* In a very large saucepan, heat the olive oil. Add the onion, carrot and garlic and cook for 10 minutes or so on a medium heat, so that the vegetables soften but do not brown.

* Add the minced beef and bacon and stir to distribute. Cook over a medium heat for about 15 minutes until brown and you can no longer see any pink meat.

* Add the tomato purée and continue to cook for 2 minutes. Then add the chicken stock and wine (if using), mix together, and allow to cook for a further 5 minutes.

* Pour in the chopped tomatoes, along with the bay leaf, salt and pepper, and stir well. Bring the heat down to low so the mixture is on a gentle simmer. Stir well and leave the mixture to cook, covered with a lid, for about an hour.

* Shortly before you're ready to eat, boil the kettle and fill a large saucepan with the boiling water. Place on a medium heat and bring back up to the boil, then add a generous pinch of salt and the spaghetti. Cook for the time stated on the packet.

* When the spaghetti is ready, drain it well in a colander. Your Bolognese sauce should also now be cooked. Mix it with the freshly cooked spaghetti and serve, sprinkled with grated Parmesan, if you like.

CREAMY BACON AND VEGETABLE PASTA BAKE

Serves: 4

A simple, delicious pasta bake with plenty of colour, texture and taste!

For the bake

400g dried pasta

200g broccoli, chopped into small florets

1 tsp olive oil

275g smoked back bacon, cut into 1cm chunks

3 garlic cloves, peeled and chopped

1 medium onion, peeled and chopped

100g mushrooms

100g mature Cheddar, grated

For the cheese sauce

50g butter

50g plain flour

700ml milk

200g mature Cheddar, grated

Salt and pepper

* Boil the kettle and fill the largest saucepan you own with the boiling water. Place on a medium heat and bring back up to the boil, then add a pinch of salt and the pasta. Cook for the time stated on the packet. Add the broccoli to the pan 5 minutes before the end of the cooking time. Once cooked, drain the pasta and broccoli well in a colander.

* In a frying pan, heat the oil over a medium heat. Add the bacon, garlic, onion and mushrooms and cook, stirring occasionally, until the onion, garlic and mushrooms are browned and softened.

* Preheat the oven to 200°C Fan/Gas Mark 7.

* Now get the cheese sauce underway. In a large saucepan, melt the butter over a low heat. While the butter is melting, make sure you have a wooden spoon, a whisk and the milk measured out in a jug next to you. Keep the pan on a gentle heat else the sauce can burn easily.

* When all of the butter is melted, tip in the flour and stir it in quickly using a wooden spoon. It will look like a thick paste. Continue to stir vigorously for the next couple of minutes until the flour and butter paste starts to bubble.

* Pour in the milk a little at a time. Whisk well after each addition and repeat. Make sure you keep whisking continuously.

* When all the milk has been added to the sauce, the sauce should look smooth and glossy. Tip in the grated cheese and continue to whisk. Season with salt and a generous amount of pepper and let it bubble away gently for 4–5 minutes. Keep whisking continuously.

* Place the cooked pasta, broccoli and bacon/mushroom mix in a large ovenproof baking dish, pour on the cheese sauce and stir together well. Sprinkle the remaining cheese over the top and bake for 20–30 minutes until golden and bubbling.

TUNA PASTA BAKE

Serves: 4

A pasta bake is the ultimate student dinner – cheap and easy, as well as warm, filling and delicious. This version is made completely with store – ingredients, so it's really simple to prepare.

400g dried pasta
2 tsp olive oil
1 large onion, peeled
and chopped
3 garlic cloves, peeled
and chopped
2 x 160–200g cans tuna, drained
400g can chopped tomatoes
100g mature Cheddar, grated
Salt and pepper

* Preheat the oven to 200°C Fan/Gas Mark 7.

* Boil the kettle and fill a large saucepan with the boiling water. Place on a medium heat and bring back up to the boil, then add a pinch of salt and the pasta. Cook for the time stated on the packet.

* In a frying pan, heat the oil, add the onion and garlic, and cook over a medium heat for a few minutes until softened.

* Add the tuna and tomatoes and stir together well. Season with salt and pepper and allow to bubble away for a few minutes.

* When the pasta is cooked, drain well in a colander and tip into a large ovenproof baking dish. Add the tuna and tomato sauce, and stir all the ingredients together thoroughly.

* Sprinkle the cheese evenly over the pasta and bake for 20–30 minutes until the cheese is really golden brown and bubbling. Serve immediately.

CHICKEN, TOMATO AND MOZZARELLA PASTA BAKE

Serves: 4

Ideal for a weeknight dinner, this tasty pasta bake has a delicious combination of ingredients and will go down well with meat-lovers. If you're feeling flush, you can also add some chorizo chunks.

400g dried pasta

2 tsp olive oil

1 onion,
peeled and chopped

3 garlic cloves,
peeled and chopped

2 boneless skinless
chicken breasts, sliced

75g chorizo chunks (optional)

500g passata

2 x 125g balls mozzarella
cheese, torn into pieces

Salt and pepper

* Boil the kettle and fill a large saucepan with the boiling water. Place on a medium heat and bring back up to the boil, then add a pinch of salt and the pasta. Cook for the time stated on the packet.

* Preheat the oven to 180°C Fan/Gas Mark 6.

* To make the tomato sauce, heat the oil in a large frying pan, add the chopped onion and cook over a medium heat for 5 minutes or so, until the onion is softened. Add the garlic and cook for another 2 minutes.

* Add the chicken (and chorizo chunks if using) and cook for 10 minutes until the pieces are no longer pink.

* Add the passata, stir well and allow the chicken to cook in the tomato sauce for a further 10 minutes, stirring occasionally.

* Once the pasta is cooked, drain well in a colander, then return it to the saucepan. Add the tomato and chicken sauce, mix well and season with salt and pepper.

* Empty half of the pasta in the bottom of a large ovenproof baking dish.

* Scatter half the mozzarella cheese evenly over the pasta, then place the remaining half of the pasta in the dish and scatter the remaining cheese over the top.

* Bake the pasta in the oven for 20–30 minutes until golden brown and bubbling.

SUPER TASTY MAC AND CHEESE WITH BACON AND LEEKS

Serves: 4

Macaroni cheese is lovely for lunch and hearty enough for dinner. This super-tasty version has some flavoursome added extras. Use the strongest mature Cheddar you can afford, to really pump up the taste.

For the filling

40g butter, plus
extra for greasing

3 medium leeks, washed
and sliced into 1cm thick rings

6 rashers of lean smoked
bacon, sliced into 1cm strips

400g dried macaroni

For the cheese sauce

50g butter

50g plain flour

700ml milk

200g mature Cheddar, grated

Salt and pepper

For the topping

50g Parmesan, finely grated

50g breadcrumbs

Tip: If you don't have any macaroni, use pasta shapes such as penne or fusilli – whatever you have in the cupboard.

* Lightly grease the base and sides of a large ovenproof dish with butter. Preheat the oven to 180°C Fan/Gas Mark 6.

* Melt the butter in a large frying pan on a low to medium heat. Add the leeks and bacon and allow to cook gently for 20 minutes or so, until the leeks are really soft but not coloured, and the bacon is well cooked.

* Meanwhile, boil the kettle and fill the largest saucepan you own with the boiling water. Place on a medium heat and bring back up to the boil, then add a pinch of salt and the macaroni and cook for 2 minutes less than the time stated on the packet. Drain well once cooked.

* Now start the cheese sauce. Make sure you have a wooden spoon, whisk and the milk measured out in a jug next to you. In a large saucepan, melt the butter on a low heat.

* When all of the butter is melted, tip in the flour and stir it in quickly using a wooden spoon. It will look like a thick paste. Continue to stir vigorously for the next couple of minutes until the flour and butter paste starts to bubble.

* Pour in the milk a little at a time, whisking vigorously after each addition until smooth.

* When all the milk has been added, the sauce should look smooth and glossy. Tip in the grated cheese and continue to whisk. Season with salt and a generous amount of pepper and let it bubble gently for 4–5 minutes, whisking continuously.

* Tip the drained macaroni, leeks, bacon and cheese sauce back into the pasta saucepan, ensuring it is dry first. Stir to combine well. Transfer the mixture to the greased baking dish. Sprinkle the Parmesan and breadcrumbs over the top.

* Bake in the oven for 30–40 minutes until the topping is golden brown and crunchy.

SPAGHETTI CARBONARA

Serves: 3–4

Carbonara is a creamy pasta sauce made with eggs and bacon.
If you've never tried making it before, you should – it's cheap and easy
to cook, but delicious enough to impress your mates. The white wine
is optional, so throw some in if you happen to have an open bottle.

10 rashers of smoked bacon

400g dried spaghetti

3 tbsp double cream

**5 tbsp finely grated Parmesan,
plus extra to serve (optional)**

2 large eggs

25g butter

**3 garlic cloves, peeled
and finely chopped**

45ml dry white wine (optional)

Salt and pepper

* Cut the bacon up into 1cm strips. Cut the fat off if you prefer. In a dry frying pan cook the bacon on a medium heat for 15 minutes or so until it's really nice and brown.

* Meanwhile, boil the kettle and fill the largest saucepan you own with the boiling water. Place on a medium heat and bring back up to the boil, then add a generous pinch of salt and the spaghetti. Cook for the time stated on the packet.

* While the bacon and spaghetti are cooking, place the cream, Parmesan and eggs into a bowl and whisk until well combined.

* When the bacon is looking nice and brown, add the butter and garlic to the frying pan and stir for a minute or so on a medium heat until you can smell the garlic cooking.

* Once the spaghetti is cooked, drain well in a colander. Make sure the saucepan you used to cook the pasta is dry before putting the well-drained spaghetti back into it. Tip in the cream, Parmesan and egg mixture and mix immediately. If you are using wine, add this now. Allow the egg mixture to begin to set (not over the hob, just in the residual heat from the pasta), for about 1–2 minutes.

* Stir in the bacon and garlic. Season with salt and pepper.

* Serve the pasta immediately with extra Parmesan grated on top, if you like.

SAUSAGE RAGÙ WITH PAPPARDELLE

Serves: 4

This is a tasty alternative to traditional Bolognese, made with sausage meat. The red wine is optional, but it makes the sauce really yummy if you do have an open bottle hanging around. The longer this sauce is cooked for, the better.

8 x 100% pork sausages

2 tbsp olive oil

1 onion, peeled and chopped finely

4 garlic cloves, peeled and chopped finely

2 tsp fennel seeds

400g can chopped tomatoes

250ml red wine (optional)

Salt and pepper

400g fresh or dried pappardelle

Parmesan, finely grated, to serve (optional)

Tip: Don't be tempted to cut corners here with cheaper sausages – they are usually bulked out with bread and rusk so you get less meat for your money. Sausages with a high meat content are tastiest.

* Slit the sausage skins open with kitchen scissors and place the sausage meat into a large bowl. Discard the skins.

* With your hands, crumble up the sausage meat so it looks like rough breadcrumbs.

* In a large frying pan, warm the oil on a medium heat.

* Add the sausage meat and cook for 10 minutes or so until the meat is browned.

* Add the onion and garlic to the sausage meat in the pan. Cook for a few minutes until they start to soften.

* Add the fennel seeds, tomatoes and wine (if using), season with salt and pepper and leave to bubble away gently for at least 45 minutes, until the ragù is thick, rich and much darker in colour.

* Shortly before you are ready to eat, boil the kettle and fill the largest saucepan you own with the boiling water. Place on a medium heat and bring back up to the boil, then add a pinch of salt and the pappardelle. Cook for the time stated on the packet. Drain well in a colander and place back in the saucepan, making sure the pan is dry first.

* Tip in the ragù, stir well to combine evenly with the pasta, and serve with a sprinkling of fresh Parmesan, if you like.

SPAGHETTI WITH GARLIC PRAWNS

Serves: 2

A lovely, light pasta dish that's quick to cook, but tastes sensational. You can buy ready-cooked prawns or even frozen ones, which are cheaper. See the Tip for defrosting them. If you fancy a glass of wine alongside this, then open a new bottle; otherwise, any leftover white wine will do.

200g dried spaghetti

25g butter

3 garlic cloves, peeled and chopped finely

1 tbsp lemon juice (from ½ a lemon)

½ tsp grated lemon zest

1 small glass (approximately 175ml) of white wine

100g cooked prawns

Parmesan, finely grated, to serve (optional)

Salt and pepper

Tip: You can quickly defrost frozen prawns by soaking them in cold water for around 15 minutes. Dry on kitchen towel before using.

* Boil the kettle and fill a large saucepan with the boiling water. Place on a medium heat and bring back up to the boil, then add a pinch of salt and the spaghetti. Cook for the time stated on the packet.

* Meanwhile, melt the butter in a frying pan over a low heat. Add the garlic and cook for 30 seconds or so until you can smell it starting to cook, but don't let it brown. Add the lemon juice, zest and wine, and stir gently to combine.

* Next, add the prawns and cook for a few minutes until they warm through.

* When the spaghetti is cooked, drain it very thoroughly in a colander. Ensure all the water has been removed from the saucepan, then tip the drained spaghetti back into the pan.

* Pour over the garlic, prawns and butter from the frying pan and return the saucepan to the heat.

* Stir the sauce through the pasta and ensure the spaghetti is well coated in sauce. Season to taste then leave to sit for 5 minutes in the pan with the lid on.

* Serve with some grated Parmesan on top, if you fancy.

SPAGHETTI AMATRICIANA

Serves: 2 generously

This traditional Italian pasta sauce of tomato, garlic and bacon is one of those dishes that sounds posh, but is actually very simple and cheap to make. It's a nice way to use up the end of a bottle of white wine, or you can just leave out the wine altogether if you prefer.

1 tbsp olive oil

1 small onion, peeled and chopped finely

2 garlic cloves, peeled and chopped finely

200g smoked bacon, sliced into 1cm strips

400g can chopped tomatoes

100ml white wine (optional)

Salt and pepper

200g dried spaghetti

Parmesan, finely grated, to serve (optional)

* In a large frying pan, warm the oil over a medium heat. Place the onion and garlic in the pan and cook for 10–15 minutes on a very low heat to allow the garlic and onion to soften, but not to brown.

* Add the strips of bacon and cook for 5 more minutes.

* Add the tomatoes and wine (if using), and season with salt and pepper. Leave to bubble away gently for at least 30 minutes.

* Boil the kettle and fill a large saucepan with the boiling water. Place on a medium heat and bring back up to the boil, then add a pinch of salt and the spaghetti. Cook for the time stated on the packet, then drain well in a colander.

* Serve the sauce piled onto a bowl of spaghetti, with a sprinkling of Parmesan on the top, if desired.

Tip: Any leftovers can easily be reheated in the microwave for a quick meal.

LASAGNE

Serves: 4

Making lasagne yourself at home is a million times better than buying a ready meal. It's a great dish for feeding a crowd – just double up the quantities and cook in a really large ovenproof dish.

For the ragù

2 tbsp olive oil

1 medium onion, peeled and finely chopped

3 cloves garlic, peeled and finely chopped

350g minced beef

400g can chopped tomatoes

2 tbsp concentrated tomato purée

1 small glass (approximately 175ml) of red wine (optional)

Salt and pepper

For the cheese sauce

15g butter

15g plain flour

300ml milk

100g very mature Cheddar or similar strongly flavoured hard cheese

Pepper

To assemble the lasagne

4–8 sheets of fresh or dried lasagne pasta (depending on the dimensions of your dish)

75g Parmesan, very mature Cheddar or similar strongly flavoured hard cheese, grated

* Start with the ragù. Heat the oil in a large saucepan on a medium heat, add the onion and cook for around 10 minutes until the onion has softened, but is not brown.

* Add the garlic and cook for a further 3–4 minutes until you can smell it cooking.

* Add the mince to the pan in chunks and break up with a wooden spoon. Keep stirring the meat until it loses its red colour.

* Add the tomatoes, tomato purée, wine (if using) and salt and pepper and stir to combine well. Leave to cook for around 20 minutes on a low heat. If you're going to eat the lasagne straight away, preheat the oven to 180°C Fan/Gas Mark 6.

* Meanwhile, start the cheese sauce. Make sure you have a wooden spoon, a whisk and the milk measured out in a jug. Melt the butter in a large saucepan on a low heat.

* When the butter is just melted, tip in the flour and stir it in quickly with the wooden spoon. It will look like a thick paste. Continue to stir vigorously over a gentle heat for the next couple of minutes until the flour and butter paste starts to bubble.

* Pour in the milk, a little bit at a time, whisking vigorously after each addition until smooth.

* When all the milk has been added, the sauce should look smooth and glossy. Tip in the grated cheese and continue to whisk. Season with pepper only and let it bubble away gently for 4–5 minutes, stirring continuously.

* When your ragù and cheese sauce are ready, you can start to assemble your lasagne. In a large baking dish, make a layer of the ragù and then add a layer of the cheese sauce. Cover with pasta sheets and start again, layering up the ragù, cheese sauce and pasta. Make sure you have a layer of pasta on the top and cover this with the grated cheese for the final layer.

* Bake in the oven for around 45 minutes until the lasagne is bubbling and the cheese on the top is golden and melted.

VODKA PASTA

Serves: 4–6 (Vegetarian)

No, it's not a typo! Vodka adds a delicious distinctive kick to this pasta sauce that's unlike anything else. You can't see or smell it in the finished dish but it tastes amazing. This is a fun recipe to cook for friends. It only needs a couple of shots of vodka, so if you don't have a bottle, maybe you can borrow some from a generous housemate.

750g cherry tomatoes, halved

Pinch of sugar

1 tsp fresh thyme

2 tbsp olive oil

2 shots (50ml) of vodka

500g dried pasta

100g mascarpone

50ml double cream

100g Parmesan (or vegetarian equivalent), finely grated, to serve

Salt and pepper

* Preheat the oven to 200°C Fan/Gas Mark 7.

* Place the tomatoes on a large baking tray. Sprinkle with salt, pepper, the sugar and thyme, and drizzle over the olive oil.

* Roast in the oven for 20–30 minutes until the tomatoes are soft and lightly browned around the edges.

* Place the vodka in a bowl, add the roasted tomatoes and stir well. Set aside.

* Boil the kettle and fill a large saucepan with the boiling water. Place on a medium heat and bring back up to the boil, then add a pinch of salt and the pasta. Cook for the time stated on the packet, then drain well in a colander. Tip back into the saucepan you cooked it in and place over a medium heat.

* Add the mascarpone cheese and cream to the pasta and stir through.

* Tip in the tomatoes and vodka and stir through well to reheat.

* Serve sprinkled with plenty of fresh Parmesan cheese.

CREAMY CHICKEN AND PESTO PASTA

Serves: 2

A lovely rich and creamy pasta sauce, which is delicious mopped up with some garlic bread. If you're a big pesto fan, feel free to add extra. And if you want to make this a little bit fancy you could even sprinkle some fresh chopped basil leaves over the top.

1 tsp olive oil

1 boneless, skinless chicken breast, chopped into 2cm chunks

200g dried pasta

6 tbsp pesto

3 tbsp double cream

Salt and pepper

Parmesan, finely grated, to serve

Handful of fresh basil leaves, chopped, to serve (optional)

Tip: If you want to add more flavour to this simple dish, why not stir some cooked green vegetables, such as peas, courgette or asparagus, into the sauce or add some chopped sun-dried tomatoes or toasted pine nuts.

* In a large saucepan, heat the oil over a medium heat. Add the chicken pieces and cook for 15–20 minutes until the chicken is cooked through.

* Meanwhile, boil the kettle and fill a large saucepan with the boiling water. Place on a medium heat and bring back up to the boil, then add a pinch of salt and the pasta. Cook for the time stated on the packet.

* While the chicken and pasta are cooking, make the sauce. In a small saucepan, cook the pesto on a low heat. Add the cream and stir well. Continue to heat the sauce until it bubbles, and then remove from the heat.

* When the pasta is cooked, drain well in a colander. Pour in the sauce, add the chicken and stir thoroughly. Season with salt and pepper, bearing in mind that you may not want to use much salt as the pesto and Parmesan are salty.

* Serve with a good sprinkling of Parmesan cheese, and a handful of chopped fresh basil leaves.

STIR-FRIES, NOODLES AND RICE

ORANGE AND LEMON CHICKEN

Serves: 2

This simple, zesty chicken is ideal for a weeknight dinner or a quick lunch. It has lovely fresh flavours and is great eaten with stir-fried green veg, steamed rice or noodles.

2 boneless skinless chicken breasts, sliced into thin strips

3 garlic cloves, peeled and crushed

3cm piece of fresh root ginger, peeled and finely grated

Grated zest and juice of 1 orange

Grated zest and juice of 1 lemon

1 tbsp soy sauce

2 tsp caster sugar

1 spring onion, finely sliced

2 tbsp sunflower or vegetable oil

Rice or noodles, to serve

* Place all the ingredients except the oil together in a bowl. Stir well, cover with cling film and leave to marinate in the fridge for an hour.

* When you are ready to cook the chicken, heat the oil in a work or large non-stick frying pan on a high heat, until it is very hot. Add the chicken mixture with all the juices.

* Stir-fry for 10–15 minutes until the chicken is cooked through. Cut open one of the largest strips to check the meat is no longer pink inside.

* Serve the cooked chicken with the sauce from the pan drizzled on top, accompanied by rice or noodles, such as special fried rice (page 45) or edamame soy noodles (page 42).

PRAWN CHOW MEIN

Serves: 4

You've probably seen chow mein on Chinese takeaway menus, but it's also a great meal to cook at home. Get stuck in and share with your mates!

250g dried egg noodles

2 tbsp sesame oil

4 spring onions, finely sliced

1 red pepper, deseeded and thinly sliced

300g raw prawns

200g beansprouts

4 tbsp soy sauce, plus extra to serve

2 tbsp sesame seeds, toasted gently in a frying pan

Rice or noodles, to serve

* Cook the egg noodles according to the packet instructions. Drain well once cooked.

* Place half the oil in a wok or large non-stick frying pan and put over a high heat until the oil is very hot.

* Add the spring onions, red pepper and prawns and cook for a minute, taking care to stir vigorously.

* Add the beansprouts and drained noodles. Pour in the soy sauce and remaining oil and stir-fry for a further 2–3 minutes until everything is heated well. Check that the prawns are pink and cooked through.

* Serve immediately with extra soy sauce and the sesame seeds sprinkled on top, and with rice or noodles alongside.

Tip: You can use frozen prawns, but make sure they are thoroughly defrosted first – soak in cold water for 15 minutes then dry on kitchen towel.

PORK, GINGER AND GARLIC STIR-FRY

Serves: 2

Don't just stick to chicken for stir-fries – pork is also very nice and not too expensive. This makes a very quick dinner out of fairly basic ingredients. Add some sliced vegetables if you like.

200g pork tenderloin, thinly sliced

2 garlic cloves, peeled and crushed

6cm piece of fresh root ginger, peeled and finely grated

2 spring onions, finely sliced

50ml soy sauce, plus extra to serve

2 tbsp sunflower or vegetable oil

1 tbsp toasted sesame seeds

* Place all the ingredients except the oil and sesame seeds together in a bowl. Stir well, cover with cling film and leave to marinate in the fridge for an hour.

* When you are ready to cook, heat the oil in a wok or non-stick frying pan on a high heat until it is very hot. Add the pork mixture and all the juices.

* Stir-fry over a high heat for around 4–5 minutes until the pork is cooked.

* Serve immediately, topped with the sesame seeds and an extra drizzle of soy sauce, if desired. Accompany with rice or noodles.

SWEET CHILLI CHICKEN STIR-FRY

Serves: 2

Sweet chilli sauce is an easy way to give a stir-fry an instant flavour boost. It goes particularly well with chicken. This is sweet and sticky and gorgeous. Feel free to add whichever vegetables you like best.

2 boneless skinless chicken breasts, sliced thinly

2 tbsp soy sauce

2 tbsp sweet chilli sauce, plus extra to serve

2 tbsp sunflower or vegetable oil

1 red pepper, deseeded and cut into thin slices

150g fresh stir-fry vegetables

* Place the sliced chicken, soy sauce and sweet chilli sauce in a bowl. Stir together, cover with cling film and leave to marinate for an hour in the fridge.

* When you are ready to cook, heat the oil in a wok or non-stick frying pan on a high heat until it is very hot. Add the chicken and sauce from the bowl and stir-fry for 5 minutes.

* Add the red pepper and vegetables and stir-fry for another 5–10 minutes until the chicken is cooked through. Cut open one of the thicker slices to check there is no pink meat inside.

* Serve immediately, with extra sweet chilli sauce on the side, accompanied by rice or noodles.

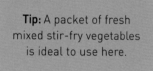

Tip: A packet of fresh mixed stir-fry vegetables is ideal to use here.

BEEF, BROCCOLI AND SPRING ONION STIR-FRY

Serves: 2

Beef is a slightly pricier option for stir-fries, so maybe save this recipe for special occasions or for when your parents are footing the supermarket bill! It is quick to make and has a savoury flavour.

300g steak (buy the best you can afford, not stewing steak)

2 garlic cloves, peeled and crushed

6cm piece of fresh root ginger, peeled and finely grated

2 spring onions, finely sliced

2 tbsp soy sauce, plus extra to serve

Grated zest and juice of 1 lime

30g brown sugar

½ tsp chilli flakes

½ head of broccoli, cut into small florets

2 tbsp sunflower or vegetable oil

Rice or noodles, to serve

* Place all the ingredients except the broccoli and oil together into a bowl. Stir well, cover with cling film and leave to marinate in the fridge for an hour.

* Meanwhile, steam, boil or microwave the broccoli until the stems are only just tender – you want to retain some crunch.

* Heat the oil in a wok or non-stick frying pan over a high heat until it is very hot. Add the steak mixture, all the liquid from the marinade and the drained broccoli.

* Stir-fry over a high heat for around 4–5 minutes until the steak is cooked.

* Serve immediately, with an extra drizzle of soy sauce, if desired, accompanied by rice or noodles, such as special fried rice (page 45) or edamame soy noodles (page 42).

PEANUT AND SESAME NOODLES

Serves: 4 (Vegetarian)

These nutty noodles go really well with any of the other stir-fry recipes in this chapter.

125g dried fine egg noodles

1 garlic clove, peeled
and crushed

2 tsp soy sauce

2 tbsp sweet chilli sauce

2 tbsp peanut butter (crunchy
or smooth are both fine)

Juice of ½ lime

3 tbsp boiling water

1 tbsp chopped
roasted peanuts

1 tbsp toasted sesame seeds

1 spring onion, finely sliced

* Cook the noodles according to the packet instructions and
  then drain well.

* While the noodles are cooking, place the garlic, soy sauce, sweet
  chilli sauce, peanut butter and lime juice together in a saucepan
  and stir well. Add the boiling water to the pan and stir over a low
  heat to loosen the sauce and warm it through.

* Add the drained noodles and stir through to evenly coat them
  in peanut sauce.

* Serve with the chopped peanuts, sesame seeds and spring
  onion scattered on top.

EDAMAME SOY NOODLES

Serves: 2 (Vegetarian)

This is good as a super-tasty and nutritious side dish, and also as a simple main course (though you might want to double the quantities). Edamame beans are cheapest bought in bags from the supermarket freezer section - they are often called soya beans instead.

100g dried egg noodles

2 garlic cloves, peeled and crushed

3cm piece of fresh root ginger, peeled and finely grated

2 spring onions, finely sliced

2 tbsp sunflower or vegetable oil

200g edamame beans

3-4 tbsp soy sauce, plus extra to serve

1 tbsp toasted sesame seeds

* Cook the noodles according to the packet instructions. Drain well once cooked.

* In a wok or non-stick frying pan, heat the oil over a high temperature until it is very hot. Add the garlic, ginger and spring onions, and cook for 2–3 minutes to soften the spring onions.

* Add the edamame beans and cooked noodles and pour in the soy sauce.

* Stir-fry over a high heat for around 2–3 minutes until the beans and noodles are piping hot.

* Serve immediately, topped with sesame seeds and with an extra drizzle of soy sauce, if desired.

Tip: Use frozen edamame (soya) beans for convenience, but defrost before use.

THAI CHICKEN AND MUSHROOM NOODLE BROTH

Serves: 2

This lovely noodle soup contains lots of veg and has a nice zingy taste from the lime juice and coriander. It's perfect for using up leftover roast chicken, and makes a great quick lunch when you're short on time. You can easily make extra to keep in a sealed container in the fridge and reheat the next day.

2 garlic cloves, peeled and finely chopped

1cm piece of fresh root ginger, peeled and finely grated

500ml hot chicken stock

¼ red chilli, finely chopped (deseeded if you prefer for less heat)

175g cooked chicken, torn into pieces (leftover roast chicken is perfect)

3 mushrooms, sliced thinly (chestnut mushrooms are good here)

½ red pepper, sliced finely

50g dried nest of noodles

1 tsp light soy sauce

1 tsp lime juice

1 tbsp chopped fresh coriander, to serve

* Place the garlic, ginger, stock and chilli into a large saucepan. Over a low heat, allow the broth to bubble away for around 15 minutes.

* Pass the broth through a sieve into a bowl and transfer the liquid back to the pan. Discard the contents of the sieve.

* Add the chicken, mushrooms, pepper and noodles to the pan, turn the heat up to medium to high and allow the broth to bubble away for another 5 minutes, until everything is heated through.

* Now, flavour the broth with the soy sauce and lime juice, to your taste. Stir well and serve in bowls with the fresh coriander sprinkled on top.

SPECIAL FRIED RICE

Serves: 4

This wallet-friendly rice dish works well as a meal on its own or is good served with any of the stir-fries in this chapter.

200g long grain rice

400ml boiling water

Pinch of salt

1 tbsp vegetable oil

2 boneless skinless chicken breasts, sliced thinly, or 200g raw prawns

3 spring onions, finely chopped

3cm piece of fresh root ginger, peeled and grated

2 garlic cloves, peeled and crushed

1 red chilli, chopped

3 tbsp frozen peas

2 large eggs, beaten

Soy sauce, to serve

* Place the rice into a large saucepan. Add the boiling water and salt, bring to the boil, cover and cook for the time stated on the packet. Drain well once cooked.

* While the rice is cooking, place the oil into a wok or a large saucepan and heat it over a high heat until it is very hot. Add the chicken or prawns and stir-fry until nearly cooked. This should take around 10 minutes if you are using chicken and 5 minutes if you are using prawns.

* Add the spring onions, ginger, garlic, chilli and peas and cook for a minute.

* Add the drained, cooked rice and then pour over the beaten egg.

* Stir the rice vigorously to distribute the egg evenly and allow it to scramble. Cook for a further 3 minutes to ensure the rice is hot enough. Serve in bowls, drizzled with soy sauce.

● ●

Tip: This recipe can also be made using leftover rice. Take it out of the fridge just before you need it. Cold rice can be a common cause of food poisoning, so keep refrigerated and use within 24 hours.

EASY PRAWN PAD THAI

Serves: 2

Pad Thai is a yummy mixture of stir-fried flat noodles, vegetables, chilli, and meat or fish. It's typically scattered with peanuts, which adds some nice crunch but isn't essential. A bottle of fish sauce keeps for ages in the fridge and is a good investment if you like making Asian dishes.

150g dried flat egg noodles

1 tbsp sunflower oil

½ red chilli, chopped finely

1 garlic clove, crushed

3cm piece of fresh root ginger, peeled and finely grated

3 spring onions, sliced finely

A handful of beansprouts

½ red pepper, thinly sliced

175g cooked prawns

2 tbsp lime juice

1 tbsp soy sauce

1 tsp fish sauce

50g chopped roasted peanuts (optional)

2 tbsp toasted sesame seeds

1 tbsp chopped fresh coriander

* Cook the noodles according to the packet instructions. Drain well once cooked.

* Heat the oil in a wok or large non-stick frying pan over a high heat until it is very hot. Add the chilli, garlic, ginger and spring onions and stir-fry for a minute or so to soften.

* Add the beansprouts, pepper, prawns and drained noodles and stir-fry for a couple of minutes to heat through.

* Pour over the lime juice, soy sauce and fish sauce and stir together to combine.

* Once all the ingredients are really hot, transfer to plates and top with the chopped peanuts (if using), sesame seeds and coriander. Serve immediately.

Tip: To make life easier, get all the chopping and grating done before you start cooking.

SOUPS, STEWS
AND CURRIES

ROASTED TOMATO SOUP

Serves: 4 (Vegetarian)

This soup is a great way to use up tomatoes that are past their best, or any that don't have much flavour – once all the other ingredients have been added, you'll never know. It's definitely not the time to splash your cash on fancy tomatoes, as you're guaranteed a good result whichever ones you use.

2 red onions, peeled and quartered

4 garlic cloves, unpeeled

650g tomatoes (large or cherry), halved

2 tsp dried basil

2 tbsp olive oil

Salt and pepper

1 litre hot vegetable stock

* Preheat the oven to 180°C Fan/Gas Mark 6.

* Place the onion, garlic and halved tomatoes in a large roasting tray.

* Sprinkle over the basil, drizzle over the olive oil and season with salt and pepper.

* Roast for 20–30 minutes until the tomatoes are soft and lightly browned around the edges and the onion is soft. Remove the skins from the garlic cloves and discard.

* Whizz the roasted tomato mixture and the stock in a blender, or place in a jug and blitz with a stick blender, until smooth. If you prefer your soup really smooth, you can pass it through a sieve. Gently reheat the soup in a saucepan before serving.

* Any leftovers can be kept in the fridge for 2–3 days or, once cooled, frozen in individual portions in freezer bags.

CHICKEN AND SWEETCORN SOUP

Serves: 4 generously

This creamy soup is hearty and filling, as well as very straightforward to make. It's a great way to use up any leftover roast chicken you might have in the fridge (see page 133 for roasting a chicken).

1 small knob of butter

**1 large onion,
peeled and finely chopped**

**2 garlic cloves, peeled
and chopped**

1 litre hot chicken stock

5 tbsp double cream

200g can sweetcorn, drained

**150g roast chicken meat,
skin and bones removed**

* Melt the butter in the largest saucepan you own. Over a medium heat, add the onion and garlic and cook gently in the melted butter for 10–15 minutes until softened, but not coloured.

* Pour the hot stock into the pan and allow to bubble away for 5 minutes or so.

* Remove from the heat and leave to cool a little, then whizz in a blender, or place in a large jug and blitz with a stick blender, until smooth.

* Pour the smooth soup back into the pan. Add the cream, sweetcorn and chicken and reheat for 5–10 minutes on a medium heat until the chicken and sweetcorn are warmed through. Serve hot.

* Any leftovers can be kept in the fridge for 2–3 days or, once cooled, frozen in individual portions in freezer bags.

MINESTRONE SOUP

Serves: 4–6

Minestrone is such a popular soup, and homemade tastes far better than canned. It's filling, chunky and full of tasty morsels. Once you add the beans and pasta, it's basically a complete meal in a bowl.

1 tbsp olive oil

1 large onion, peeled and finely chopped

3 garlic cloves, peeled and finely chopped

1 leek, washed and sliced into thin rings

1 large carrot, peeled and cut into 1cm dice

2 medium courgettes, cut into 1cm dice

2 rashers of smoked bacon, cut into 1cm strips

2 x 400g cans chopped tomatoes

400g can cannellini beans, drained and rinsed

100g kale or cabbage, chopped into small pieces, with any tough bits removed

100g small dried pasta shapes

1.3 litres hot chicken stock

1 piece of Parmesan rind (optional)

Salt and pepper

* Heat the oil in a large saucepan. Add the onion, garlic and leek and allow to cook over a medium heat for around 10 minutes until softened and the onion is slightly translucent.

* Add the carrot, courgette and bacon and cook for a further 5 minutes, stirring continuously.

* Add the tomatoes, beans and kale or cabbage, and stir well.

* Next, add the pasta shapes, hot stock, Parmesan rind, if using, and salt and pepper. Stir and allow to simmer for 45 minutes, covered with a lid, before removing the Parmesan rind and serving.

* Any leftovers can be kept in the fridge for 2–3 days or, once cooled, frozen in individual portions in freezer bags.

TUSCAN VEGETABLE SOUP
To make a delicious Tuscan vegetable soup, simply follow the above recipe, omitting the bacon, beans and pasta. Use vegetable stock instead of chicken to make it suitable for vegetarians.

Tip: If you buy Parmesan cheese, save the rind for this soup. Otherwise, supermarket delis will often give you the rind for free or next to nothing.

QUICK PEA AND HAM SOUP

Serves: 4

This soup is big on flavour and bright in colour! Frozen peas are perfectly good here – it's best to spend your money on some decent ham instead. This is quick to make and can be taken from cupboard to table in under half an hour.

50g butter

1 small onion, peeled and chopped fairly finely

450g frozen peas

750ml hot chicken stock

1 bay leaf

200g thick ham or gammon, torn or chopped

4 tbsp cream, crème fraîche or full-fat yoghurt

Salt and pepper

Tip: Try to use the best ham you can for this recipe – ideally buy a thick slice of ham or gammon from a butcher or supermarket counter. Thinly sliced ham will not work well.

* Melt the butter in a large saucepan. Add the onion and cook gently over a medium heat for 5–10 minutes until the onion is softened and slightly translucent, but not browned.

* Add the peas and stir well, followed by the stock, bay leaf and salt and pepper. Stir again and leave to bubble away for 10 minutes until the peas are tender.

* Remove the bay leaf and whizz the soup in a blender, or place in a large jug and blitz with a stick blender, until smooth.

* Add the ham and the cream, crème fraîche or yoghurt, whichever you are using, and stir well.

* Taste the soup to check the seasoning, add more salt and pepper if you wish, and serve immediately.

* Any leftovers can be kept in the fridge for 2–3 days or, once cooled, frozen in individual portions in freezer bags.

SPICY SQUASH AND CHICKPEA SOUP

Serves: 4 (Vegetarian)

Thick and nutritious, a bowl of this hearty soup for lunch will keep you going all afternoon. If you aren't a fan of spicy food you can simply leave out the chilli flakes to make it milder.

1 tbsp olive oil

1 large onion, peeled and chopped

2 garlic cloves, peeled and chopped

1 medium squash (about 800g whole), peeled, deseeded and cut into cubes

1 bay leaf

1 tsp dried thyme

1 tsp ground cumin

1 tsp chilli flakes

1 tsp ground cinnamon

400g tin chickpeas, drained and rinsed

1 litre vegetable stock

* In the largest saucepan you own (ensure it has a well-fitting lid), heat the olive oil. Add the onion and garlic, and cook over a medium heat for around 5 minutes until softened and fragrant, but not coloured.

* Add the squash, herbs and spices and chickpeas. Stir together well so that the spices are evenly distributed.

* Pour in the stock, stir, cover and allow the soup to bubble away gently for around 1½ hours. The soup needs to cook slowly so that the squash and chickpeas are really tender.

* Whizz in a blender, or place in a large jug and blitz with a stick blender, until smooth. Reheat if necessary and serve with some bread for dunking.

* Any leftovers can be kept in the fridge for 2–3 days or, once cooled, frozen in individual portions in freezer bags.

BACON AND LENTIL SOUP

Serves: 4

This is a really satisfying soup – the lentils make it nice and filling, and the bacon adds loads of flavour. This recipe makes plenty, so it will keep you fed for a couple of days or you can freeze it in individual portions, then defrost and reheat in the microwave another time.

1 tbsp olive oil

1 large onion, peeled and chopped into 1cm dice

2 garlic cloves, peeled and chopped

2 large carrots, peeled and cut into 1cm dice

2 celery sticks, sliced into pieces 1cm thick

6 rashers of smoked back bacon, cut into strips

175g cooked puy lentils, from a pouch or drained and rinsed if from a can

400g can chopped tomatoes

1 bay leaf

750ml chicken stock

* Heat the olive oil in the largest saucepan you own, add the onion, garlic, carrot and celery and cook on a medium heat for around 10 minutes until softened.

* Add the bacon and cook for a further 5 minutes until brown.

* Now, add the lentils, tomatoes, bay leaf and chicken stock.

* Leave the soup to simmer away for an hour with the lid on. Then serve, with crusty bread if you like.

* Any leftovers can be kept in the fridge for 2–3 days or, once cooled, frozen in individual portions in freezer bags.

CARROT AND CORIANDER SOUP

Serves: 4 (Vegetarian)

A steaming bowl of this mildly spiced soup is nutritious, full of flavour and costs next to nothing to make.

1 tbsp olive oil

1 large onion,
peeled and chopped

450g carrots, peeled
and sliced

1 tsp ground coriander

1.2 litres vegetable stock

A squeeze of lemon juice

Salt and pepper

* Heat the oil in a large frying pan. Add the onion and carrots and cook over a medium heat until they are softened, but take care they do not brown.

* Add the ground coriander and the stock and bring to the boil. Cover and simmer for around 20 minutes or until the carrot is really tender.

* Whizz in a blender, or place in a jug and blitz with a stick blender, until smooth. Then add the lemon juice and season with salt and pepper. Gently reheat the soup in a saucepan before serving.

* Any leftovers can be kept in the fridge for 2–3 days or, once cooled, frozen in individual portions in freezer bags.

VEGETABLE HONEY TAGINE

Serves: 4 (Vegetarian)

This vegetarian recipe turns humble chickpeas into a rich and delicious stew. Cooked slowly with a mix of spices and honey, they absorb loads of gorgeous flavour. It doesn't need to cook for as long as a meat tagine (see page 60) or the chickpeas and veg will break down completely – you do want them to keep their shape.

1 tsp olive oil

3 garlic cloves,
peeled and finely chopped

2.5cm piece of fresh root ginger,
peeled and finely grated

1 tsp cumin seeds

2 tsp paprika

2 tsp ground cinnamon

2 tsp tomato purée

400g can chopped tomatoes

400g can chickpeas,
drained and rinsed

3 red peppers, deseeded and
chopped into 2cm chunks

2 large courgettes, sliced
into pieces 1cm thick

A handful of sultanas (optional)

200ml vegetable stock

2 tsp honey

4 tsp lemon juice

Salt and pepper

Couscous, to serve

* Heat the oil in a large saucepan over a medium heat. Add the garlic and ginger, and cook for a few moments until they are softened and aromatic.

* Add the spices and cook for a further minute, stirring continuously.

* Next, add the tomato purée, chopped tomatoes, chickpeas, peppers, courgettes and sultanas, if you are using them, then stir all the ingredients together to combine evenly.

* Add the vegetable stock and honey and allow to cook for around 30 minutes, covered with a lid. Give the tagine a stir every 5 minutes or so.

* Check the vegetables are tender. If they are, you're ready to serve. If not, allow the tagine to cook for another 10 minutes and check again.

* When the tagine is cooked, finish by adding the lemon juice and seasoning with salt and pepper. Serve with couscous.

LAMB TAGINE

Serves: 4

A tagine is a rich, spiced stew that's full of intense flavours. It's cooked for a long time on a low heat, so the lamb absorbs loads of flavour and becomes so tender that it pretty much falls apart when you eat it. It's very good served with couscous and a dollop of plain yoghurt.

3 tbsp olive oil

600g lamb shoulder, cubed

2 large onions, peeled and chopped

4 carrots, peeled and chopped

2 garlic cloves, peeled and finely chopped

2 tbsp ras-el-hanout (optional, see Tip)

2 tsp ground ginger

800ml lamb stock

400g can chopped tomatoes

3 star anise

2 cinnamon sticks

250g soft dried prunes, stoned

Handful of sultanas

400g can chickpeas, drained and rinsed

Salt

Couscous, to serve

* Heat the oil in a large saucepan or cast-iron casserole dish with a lid on a medium to high heat. Brown the lamb in the oil until golden brown.

* Add the onion and carrot and fry over a medium heat until they start to soften. Add the garlic, ras-el-hanout and ginger and fry for a few minutes, stirring constantly.

* Next, add the stock, tomatoes, star anise and cinnamon. Stir, bring to the boil, then cover and simmer over a low heat for 45 minutes.

* Add the prunes, sultanas and chickpeas, season with salt and simmer further, for a minimum of 30 minutes, or up to 1 hour if you have the time, as this intensifies the flavours.

* Serve the freshly made tagine with couscous. If you want to make it extra special, top with Greek yoghurt, fresh coriander and toasted flaked almonds.

Tip: Ras-el-hanout is a North African blend of spices, including cinnamon, nutmeg, cloves and pepper. It is becoming available in supermarkets or can be bought online.

CHILLI CON CARNE

Serves: 4

When you're feeding lots of people, chilli con carne always does the job, but it's also ideal to cook for yourself and keep the extra in the freezer. Adjust the chilli powder depending on how much spice you like. Serve with rice, on a jacket potato or with garlic bread.

1 tbsp olive oil

1 onion, peeled
and chopped finely

3 garlic cloves, peeled
and chopped finely

500g minced beef

1 tsp ground cumin

1 tsp ground coriander

1 tsp ground cinnamon

1 tsp hot chilli powder

2 beef stock cubes

400g can red kidney beans,
drained and rinsed

400g can chopped tomatoes

3 tbsp tomato purée

Salt and pepper

Rice, to serve

* In a large frying pan, heat the oil on a medium temperature. Add the onion and garlic to the pan and cook for 5–10 minutes until they are softened but not browned. Watch that the heat does not get too high.

* Next, add the mince. Break it up using a wooden spoon so that it is in even chunks. Allow the meat to cook for 10 minutes or so until it is browned. If any water comes out of the meat, allow it to cook off before moving on to the next stage of the recipe.

* Add the cumin, coriander, cinnamon and chilli powder and crumble in the beef stock cubes. Stir well.

* Next, add the kidney beans and tomatoes, including the juice in the can, and finally the tomato purée. Stir well and season with salt and pepper.

* Leave the chilli to bubble away gently, covered with a lid, for a minimum of 20 minutes before serving with rice.

Tip: Any leftovers freeze well. This chilli is also very easy to reheat in the microwave for a quick meal another day.

PORK CASSEROLE WITH DUMPLINGS

Serves: 4

A casserole is real comfort food for cold weather. It's nice to include caraway here, which has a mild aniseed taste and is particularly lovely in the dumplings, but it's not essential if you want to leave it out. This is great served with a glass of red wine if you're looking for a use for the rest of the bottle, else just use any leftover wine you might have hanging around.

For the casserole

1 tbsp olive oil

500g pork shoulder, cut into chunks

2 medium onions, peeled and cut into chunks

2 red peppers, deseeded and cut into large chunks

3 garlic cloves, peeled and chopped

2 tbsp tomato purée

1 tsp sweet paprika

Pinch of cayenne pepper

1 tsp caraway seeds (optional)

500ml hot beef stock

250ml red wine

1 bay leaf

Salt and pepper

For the dumplings

125g self-raising flour

2 tsp caraway seeds (optional)

50g suet

3 tbsp cold water

Salt and pepper

* In the largest saucepan you have (ensure it has a well-fitting lid), heat the olive oil on a medium–high heat. Add the pork chunks and cook for a few minutes until lightly browned.

* Add the onion, peppers and garlic, followed by the tomato purée, paprika, cayenne pepper and caraway seeds if using. Stir together well.

* Now, add the beef stock, wine, bay leaf and salt and pepper. Stir again and cover. Leave the casserole to bubble away gently over a medium heat for at least 1½ hours. You can leave it for up to 2 hours if you have enough time, and the meat will become really tender.

* While the casserole is cooking, make the dumplings. Place the flour, caraway seeds if using, suet and salt and pepper together in a mixing bowl. Stir together to combine.

* Add the cold water, little by little, to bring the mixture together to form a soft and slightly sticky dough. Be careful that the dumplings do not become soggy, so take care to add the water gradually, as you may not need it all.

* Pinch off pieces of the dough and roll into golf ball-sized dumplings. Set aside.

* About 20 minutes before you are ready to eat, add the dumplings to the top of the casserole. Cook for a further 20 minutes and serve the casserole and dumplings with green vegetables.

BEEF CASSEROLE

Serves: 4

Make this hearty casserole for friends or even just all for yourself. It keeps really well, and in fact improves after a couple of days. Ideally, use stewing beef, which is much cheaper than steak but does have to be cooked for plenty of time to make it tender. This recipe uses half a bottle of wine, so it's worth opening a bottle for.

2 tbsp plain flour

3 tbsp olive oil

600g stewing steak or shin of beef, cut into chunks

2 large onions, peeled and cut lengthways into 8

325ml hot beef stock

2 large carrots, peeled and each cut into 8 chunky slices

325ml red wine or stout

Either 100g sliced mushrooms, 2 small turnips cut into 2cm chunks or 3 large parsnips, peeled and each cut into 8 chunky slices

1 bay leaf

1 tsp fresh or dried thyme leaves

Salt and pepper

Potatoes, mashed or boiled, to serve

* Place the flour onto a large plate. Season with salt and pepper and stir well.

* Heat 2 tablespoons of the oil in a large saucepan on a medium temperature.

* Place the stewing steak a few chunks at a time into the flour. Toss well to ensure each chunk is well covered and then place the meat into the pan.

* When all the chunks of beef have been floured and are in the pan, turn up the heat to brown the beef chunks well. You may need a little extra oil to stop the meat from sticking.

* Once the beef chunks are browned, remove them from the pan and set aside on a plate.

* Add the remaining tablespoon of oil to the pan and stir in the onions. Cook over a medium heat for 5 minutes until they soften slightly. Pour in half the beef stock and stir well. This is to incorporate any flavours and juices on the bottom of the pan.

* Return the meat to the pan, followed by the remaining stock, carrot, wine or stout, your choice of other vegetables, the bay leaf and the thyme leaves.

* Season with salt and pepper, stir well and allow to simmer over a gentle heat, covered with a lid, for at least 2 hours.

* Serve with mashed or boiled potatoes and a side of vegetables.

SAUSAGE CASSEROLE

Serves: 4

Sausages make a brilliant casserole, cooked in a delicious tomato sauce with onions, garlic and herbs. The red wine isn't essential here but does make the sauce much richer – just throw in any you might have left over. Full of flavour, this is perfect on a chilly day, served with crusty bread or mash.

2 tbsp olive oil

8 large pork sausages

4 rashers of smoked bacon, cut into 1cm strips

1 large onion, peeled and cut into 5mm thick rings

2 garlic cloves, peeled and chopped finely

50g mushrooms, chopped

400g can chopped tomatoes

250ml chicken stock

1 small glass (approximately 175ml) red wine (optional)

Herbs of your choice, such as dried mixed herbs, or fresh rosemary, thyme or bay leaves

Salt and pepper

Mashed potato and vegetables, to serve

* Preheat the oven to 180°C Fan/Gas Mark 6.

* In a large frying pan, heat 1 tablespoon of the oil on a medium to high heat. Add the sausages and bacon and cook until they are browned. This should take around 10 minutes.

* Once the sausages and bacon are browned, remove them from the pan, place in a large ovenproof baking dish and set aside.

* Warm the second tablespoon of olive oil in the frying pan, add the onion and garlic and cook over a medium heat until softened. Make sure the temperature is not too high.

* Add the mushrooms, tomatoes, stock and wine (if using) to the onion and garlic, and stir well.

* Season with salt and pepper and your herbs of choice.

* Stir frequently until the sauce is bubbling and then transfer to the baking dish with the bacon and sausages and stir together.

* Bake in the oven for 30–40 minutes until the sauce is thicker, the sausages are cooked through and the mushrooms are nice and soft.

* Serve immediately with mashed potato and a side of vegetables.

Tip: Use the best-quality sausages you can afford here, but don't go for flavoured ones.

BEEF IN BEER

Serves: 4

Cooking beef in beer makes it really tender and gives it a lovely rich flavour. This recipe is best made with stewing beef, which is much cheaper than steak but does have to be cooked for plenty of time so that it's not tough. And go for a light ale rather than a dark one, or the sauce will be far too strong.

1 tbsp olive oil

400g stewing steak or shin of beef, cut into chunks

2 large onions, peeled and each cut into 8

300g mushrooms, sliced

1 tbsp plain flour

450ml light ale

1 beef stock cube

1 sprig of fresh thyme or 1 tsp dried thyme

2 garlic cloves, peeled and crushed

Salt and pepper

Mashed potato, to serve

* Preheat the oven to 140°C Fan/Gas Mark 3.

* Heat the oil in a large frying pan over a high heat. Add the meat and cook until browned. Once browned, remove from the pan and place on a plate.

* Add the onions and mushrooms to the pan and cook for a few minutes, again on a high heat, until browned.

* Transfer the browned meat, onions and mushrooms into a large saucepan with a tight-fitting lid. Add the flour and stir through.

* Add the ale, crumble in the stock cube and add the thyme and garlic. Stir well and season with salt and pepper. Bring the liquid up to a simmer.

* Leave the casserole to bubble away gently for 2–2½ hours, keeping the lid on and stirring occasionally. Serve with mashed potato and vegetables.

BOMBAY POTATO CURRY

Serves: 2 as a main or 4 as a side (Vegetarian)

This curry makes such a tasty vegetarian dinner, and is also good served as a side dish to help a meat curry go further. The potatoes are tossed in a spicy butter, which makes them taste really amazing!

300g small waxy potatoes, such as Charlotte variety

2 tbsp sunflower, rapeseed or vegetable oil

1 tbsp mustard seeds

½ tsp ground cumin

1 tsp ground turmeric

1 tsp garam masala

1 tsp chilli powder

5cm piece of fresh root ginger, peeled and finely chopped

40g butter

200g fresh or canned tomatoes, roughly chopped

Salt and pepper

* Wash the potatoes and place them whole, with their skins on, into a saucepan filled with cold water. Bring the water up to the boil and parboil the potatoes for 12–15 minutes until you can just start to insert a knife into them. Drain and cut the potatoes into quarters lengthways.

* Heat the oil in a large frying pan.

* Add the spices and fry gently over a medium heat until you can start to smell the spices cooking. Be very careful not to let them burn – if in doubt, take the pan off the heat.

* When the spices are lightly fried and smelling aromatic, add the ginger and butter to the pan and melt gently with the spices over a low heat.

* Add the potato quarters to the butter and spices in the frying pan. Turn the hob up to a medium heat and let the potatoes sizzle away in the butter and spices for 15 minutes. Make sure they are completely coated in the spicy butter and keep an eye on the temperature – you don't want the butter to burn, which it will do if the hob is too hot.

* Finally, add the tomatoes, salt and pepper and let the potatoes bubble away gently for a further 15 minutes. Serve on its own, or as a side dish with a meat curry and rice.

SIMPLE CHICKEN CURRY

Serves: 4

Homemade curry recipes often include loads of obscure ingredients, but this one is simple, cheap and student-friendly. Don't be put off by fenugreek and turmeric – you can get them in the supermarket, or even leave them out if you have to. This is really delicious, and much healthier than a takeaway curry, too!

2 tsp ground fenugreek

2 tsp ground turmeric

2 tsp cumin seeds

2 tsp coriander seeds

2 tsp chilli powder or 1 fresh red chilli, chopped finely (discard the seeds if you prefer your curry milder)

2 tbsp sunflower oil

1 onion, peeled and chopped finely

4 garlic cloves, peeled and chopped finely

6cm piece of fresh root ginger, peeled and grated very finely

4 boneless skinless chicken breasts, cut into 2–3cm chunks

400g can chopped tomatoes

400ml can coconut milk

Pilau rice (page 161), to serve

Naan bread, to serve

* Place the spices and chilli powder, if using rather than fresh chilli, into a non-stick frying pan and fry them without oil for a minute or two until you can smell the spices. Remove from the heat so the spices do not burn and place in a bowl to cool slightly.

* In the same pan, heat the oil gently. Add the onion, garlic, ginger and fresh chilli, if using, and cook over a gentle heat for 10–15 minutes until the onion is softened. Do not allow any of the ingredients to brown, so keep the heat on the hob low.

* Meanwhile, grind the cooled spices into a powder using a pestle and mortar or coffee grinder. If you don't have either, simply place the spices in a plastic food bag and crush them using a rolling pin or the bottom of a wine bottle.

* Add the chicken and crushed spices to the pan and cook for a further 10 minutes, still on a low heat.

* Add the chopped tomatoes and coconut milk and cook for another 30 minutes or so until the sauce has thickened.

* Serve with pilau rice (page 161) and naan bread.

* This curry will keep for up to 3 days in the fridge if you have any leftovers. It will also freeze well.

QUICK THAI RED CURRY

Serves: 2

Thai curry is incredibly simple to cook, with the ingredients basically left to simmer away in a spicy coconut broth. If this is more than you can eat in one sitting, it can be kept in the fridge and reheated in the microwave. Serve with coconut rice (below).

1 tbsp sunflower oil

2 boneless skinless chicken breasts, cut into chunks

Approx 2 tbsp Thai red curry paste (check the instructions on the jar as brands vary)

200ml coconut milk

1 red pepper, deseeded and cut into 1cm strips

150g green beans, ends cut off if fresh (frozen are also fine though)

Salt and pepper

* In a large saucepan heat the oil on a medium temperature. As it starts to warm up, add the chunks of chicken and fry them for around 5–10 minutes until each chunk is very lightly browned on all sides.

* Add the curry paste and stir through evenly. Allow it to cook for 2–3 minutes while stirring continuously. Add the coconut milk, cover and let the curry bubble away gently for 10 minutes or so.

* Uncover, stir well and add the pepper and beans. Cook for another 5 minutes until the vegetables are cooked through. If you are using frozen green beans, you may need to cook for around another 2 minutes until the beans are tender.

* Season with salt and pepper. Serve with rice and fresh lime wedges.

COCONUT RICE

Serves: 2 (Vegetarian)

This is an easy way to make plain rice more interesting – perfect with a Thai curry.

120g basmati rice

85ml coconut milk

250ml boiling water

Pinch of salt

1 tsp sugar

1 tbsp sesame seeds

* Place the rice, coconut milk, boiling water, salt and sugar together into a saucepan and bring to the boil.

* Cover with a lid and simmer away for around 12 minutes until the rice is tender and cooked through.

* Meanwhile, place the sesame seeds in a dry frying pan over a medium heat and cook for a couple of minutes until you can start to smell them. Remove from the heat before the seeds begin to colour.

* Sprinkle the rice with the toasted sesame seeds, to serve.

CREAMY FISH CURRY

Serves: 4

Fish works brilliantly in a curry and is a much lighter option than meat. It is also quicker to cook. The coconut milk makes this smooth and quite mild. Don't be put off by the fenugreek and turmeric – you can get them in the supermarket, or even leave them out if you have to. This is delicious with rice and a generous dollop of mango chutney.

For the paste

6 garlic cloves, peeled

5cm piece of fresh root ginger, peeled and sliced

1 chilli, red or green, deseeded

1 heaped tsp ground coriander

Generous pinch of ground turmeric

A generous pinch of ground cumin

1 tsp vegetable oil

For the curry

1 tbsp vegetable oil

1 tsp fenugreek seeds

1 large onion, peeled and finely sliced

200ml coconut milk

500g any white fish, skinned, boned and cut into large chunks (5–6 cm)

Salt and pepper

Rice, to serve

* Place all the ingredients for the paste together into a food processor or blender. Blitz until you have a smooth paste. You may need to scrape down the sides and blitz again. If you don't have a food processor, chop all the paste ingredients together really finely, leaving out the oil. You could also pound the finely chopped ingredients using a pestle and mortar, if you have one.

* To cook the curry, heat the oil in a large saucepan over a medium to high heat. Add the prepared paste and fenugreek seeds and cook for a minute or two.

* Add the onion, coconut milk and fish. Season well with salt and pepper.

* Allow the curry to cook for 10–15 minutes until the fish is cooked through. Serve with rice.

FIFTEEN-MINUTE CHICKPEA CURRY

Serves: 4 (Vegetarian)

A meat-free curry is a great veggie dish, but also makes a simple, cheap dinner for meat-eaters. This recipe uses mainly canned or store-cupboard ingredients, and as the name suggests, it can be on the table really quickly.

2 tsp olive oil

1 medium onion, peeled and diced

3 garlic cloves, peeled and finely chopped

2 tsp freshly grated root ginger

1 tsp ground cinnamon

1 tbsp curry powder

1 tsp cumin seeds

2 x 400g cans chickpeas, drained and rinsed

400g can chopped tomatoes

3 tbsp tomato purée

Salt and pepper

Rice, to serve

Naan bread or flatbread, to serve

Handful of fresh coriander leaves, to serve (optional)

* In a large saucepan, heat the oil. Add the onion, garlic and ginger and cook over a medium heat for a minute or two until the garlic and ginger are softened and fragrant.

* Add the cinnamon, curry powder and cumin seeds and cook for a minute, stirring continuously.

* Add the chickpeas, chopped tomatoes and tomato purée and cook for 10 minutes over a medium to high heat, ensuring the liquid is bubbling away gently.

* Season with salt and pepper and serve with rice, naan breads or flatbreads and some fresh coriander if you have any.

JACKET
POTATOES
AND TOPPINGS

OVEN-BAKED JACKET POTATO

Serves: 1 (Vegetarian)

The humble jacket potato makes a great standby meal, as well as being one of the best comfort foods known to man! Keep a potato or two in the cupboard to ensure you always have a quick dinner to hand. Oven-baked jacket potatoes are especially good because of their crispy skins. Add whatever fillings or toppings you fancy (see pages 78–83 for ideas).

**1 baking potato
(check the variety you buy
is suitable for baking)
2 large pinches of salt**

Tip: Make sure you keep your potatoes in a dark cupboard. Don't leave them out on the counter or in a fruit bowl or they will start to sprout. Don't keep raw potatoes in the fridge.

* Preheat the oven to 220°C Fan/Gas mark 9.

* With a sharp knife prick your potato five or six times all over. This will prevent it from potentially exploding in the oven!

* Wash your potato well and shake off the excess water.

* While the potato skin is still slightly damp, sprinkle the salt over the potato and rub it all over the skin.

* Bake the potato directly on the oven shelf for around 50–75 minutes, depending on the size of your potato.

* Test if the potato is done by sticking a sharp knife into it to see how soft it feels. The knife should easily slip into the potato when it is cooked enough. The skin should also feel crisp to the touch. If it's not quite cooked, bake for a further 10 minutes and test again.

* Serve immediately with your topping of choice (see the following pages for ideas).

MICROWAVED JACKET POTATO

Serves: 1 (Vegetarian)

If you're in a hurry, jacket potatoes can also be done in the microwave. They won't have a crispy skin like oven-baked ones, but they'll be ready in a fraction of the time. Add whatever fillings or toppings you fancy (see pages 78–83 for ideas).

1 baking potato (check the variety you buy is suitable for baking)

* Wash your potato well and dry thoroughly.

* With a sharp knife prick your potato five or six times all over. This will prevent it from potentially exploding in the microwave!

* Place the potato on a microwaveable plate and cook for 4 minutes on high for a small potato, or 6 minutes on high for a large potato.

* Turn the potato over and cook, again on high, for another 4–6 minutes, depending on the size. A small potato may take 8 minutes in total, a large potato may take 12 minutes.

* Test if the potato is done by sticking a sharp knife into it to see how soft it feels. The knife should easily slip into the potato when it is cooked enough. If it's not quite cooked, microwave for a further 2 minutes and test again.

* Serve immediately with your topping of choice (see the following pages for ideas).

JACKET POTATO TOPPINGS:

PRAWNS AND MARIE ROSE SAUCE

Serves: 1

1 tsp mayonnaise

½ tsp tomato ketchup

¼ tsp lemon juice

50g cooked prawns

Salt and pepper

1 freshly cooked jacket potato

* Place the mayonnaise, ketchup, lemon juice and salt and pepper in a bowl and mix well to combine.

* Add the prawns and stir in.

* Serve immediately on top of a jacket potato.

CREAMY MUSHROOMS

Serves: 1 (Vegetarian)

20g butter

1 garlic clove, peeled and chopped finely

1 large mushroom or 3–4 small mushrooms, sliced 5mm thick

2 tbsp cream, full-fat crème fraîche or full-fat cream cheese

Salt and pepper

1 freshly cooked jacket potato

Finely chopped chives and herbs

* Melt the butter in a small saucepan over a medium heat.

* Add the chopped garlic and cook for a minute or two until you can smell the garlic cooking.

* Add the mushrooms and allow them to cook for 10 minutes or so until soft. Pour away any excess water that has come out of the mushrooms.

* Add the cream, crème fraîche, or cream cheese and stir well to combine with the mushrooms. Season with salt and pepper and spoon on top of the jacket potato.

* Garnish with the chives and herbs and serve immediately.

SMOKED MACKEREL PÂTÉ

Serves: 1

40g smoked mackerel fillet
(approximately ½ a fillet)

30g cream cheese

½ tsp lemon juice

Salt and pepper

1 freshly cooked jacket potato

* Place the mackerel in a bowl and flake well using a fork. Ensure all bones and skin have been removed.

* Add the cream cheese and mash both ingredients well. This will make a rough pâté. If you'd prefer it smoother and have a blender or food processor, you can blitz this for around 30 seconds to create a smoother texture.

* Add the lemon juice, salt and pepper and mix well. Serve immediately on top of a jacket potato.

PESTO ROASTED VEGETABLES AND MOZZARELLA

Serves: 1 (Vegetarian)

50g Roasted Mediterranean
Vegetables (page 151) or frozen
chargrilled veg, defrosted

1 tsp pesto

1 freshly cooked jacket potato

50g fresh mozzarella
(roughly ½ a ball)

* Preheat the grill.

* Place the roasted vegetables in a small saucepan over a medium heat.

* Add the pesto and stir through the vegetables. Feel free to add more if you like. The vegetables and pesto will be warmed through after 4–5 minutes.

* Cut your cooked jacket potato in half and place the vegetables on top, followed by strips of mozzarella cheese.

* Place under the grill for 3–4 minutes until the mozzarella is melted. Enjoy immediately.

Tip: You can buy bags of frozen chargrilled Mediterranean veg in supermarkets, or else this is a great way to use up leftovers.

CHEESE AND LEEKS

Serves: 1 (Vegetarian)

1 tsp butter

½ leek, washed and
sliced into 5mm rings

1 freshly cooked jacket potato

50g grated Cheddar cheese

Pepper

* If you've used the oven to bake your potato, make sure
  you leave it on once the potato is cooked – but turn down
  to 200°C Fan/Gas mark 7.

* Gently melt the butter in a saucepan. Add the leek and cook
  gently over a medium heat for around 15 minutes, so that the
  leek rings soften well.

* Slice the cooked potato carefully in half. Scoop the fluffy
  potato out of the skin (taking care not to damage the skin)
  and place in a bowl. Place the skins on a baking sheet and
  set aside.

* If you used the microwave to cook your potato, preheat the
  grill now.

* Add the cooked leek and half the cheese to the potato flesh
  and mix well.

* Spoon the potato mixture back into the potato skins and
  sprinkle with the remaining cheese and some pepper.

* Place the baking sheet in the oven and bake for 15–20 minutes,
  or grill for 8–10 minutes, until the cheese topping is golden
  and bubbling.

BACON, MUSHROOM AND SOURED CREAM

Serves: 1

½ tsp olive oil

2 rashers of bacon, cut into 1cm strips

3–4 small mushrooms, sliced 5mm thick

1 freshly cooked jacket potato

2 tsp soured cream

Pepper

* In a small frying pan, heat the oil. Add the bacon and mushrooms and cook over a medium heat for around 10 minutes or until they are cooked through. The bacon should be lightly browned.

* Cut open your cooked potato and place the bacon and mushroom filling on the top. Spoon over the soured cream and add a sprinkle of black pepper. Enjoy immediately.

TUNA, PEPPER AND RED ONION

Serves: 1

Canned tuna, drained (use ½ a can or a whole can, depending on your appetite)

½ pepper (any colour), cut into 1cm squares

¼ red onion, peeled and sliced very thinly

1 tsp mayonnaise

Salt and pepper

1 freshly cooked jacket potato

* Place the drained tuna in a bowl and add the pepper and onion.

* Add the mayonnaise, salt and pepper and stir well.

* Serve on top of your jacket potato.

HOUMOUS AND ROASTED PEPPERS

Serves: 1 (Vegetarian)

50g roasted peppers (page 161)
1 freshly cooked jacket potato
1 tbsp houmous, ready-made or see page 115

* Warm the roasted peppers by placing them in a non-stick frying pan over a medium heat, stirring frequently, for 3–4 minutes.

* Cut open your jacket potato and top with the houmous and peppers.

Tip: You can buy bags of frozen roasted Mediterranean veg in supermarkets, or else this is a great use for leftovers.

STEAK AND ONION

Serves: 1

50–100g cooked or raw steak (you can use any cut you like)
1 tsp olive oil
1 medium onion, peeled and cut into 5mm thick rings
Salt and pepper
1 freshly cooked jacket potato

* If you are using leftover cooked steak, simply slice thinly and set aside. To cook raw steak, cut into thin strips and season with salt and pepper. Set aside.

* Heat the olive oil in a frying pan, add the onion and cook for around 10 minutes on a medium heat until the onion rings become translucent.

* If you are cooking the steak from raw, add it to the pan now and cook until the steak is as you like it. For medium-well done it's 3–4 minutes. Cook for a minute more for well done and a minute less for medium-rare.

* Cut open the jacket potato and serve the onions and steak on top with some extra salt and pepper.

Tip: This is a great way to use up leftover steak, or just ask the butcher to give you a tiny piece of raw steak, cut to the weight you want.

EASY
DINNERS

FETA AND SPINACH FRITTATA

Serves: 2 (Vegetarian)

A frittata is a kind of chunky omelette that is cooked in a frying pan. Keep some spinach in the freezer and a packet of feta in the fridge so you can rustle this up when you get back late from lectures.

100g spinach leaves, fresh or frozen

25g butter

6 large eggs

75g feta cheese

Pepper

Grated nutmeg (optional)

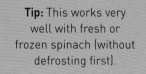

Tip: This works very well with fresh or frozen spinach (without defrosting first).

* If you are using fresh spinach leaves, wash well and shake dry.

* Melt the butter in a non-stick frying pan over a medium heat. Add the fresh or frozen spinach leaves, stir well and allow them to soften and wilt in the butter. Fresh leaves will shrink dramatically and turn a darker green after 2–3 minutes, while frozen leaves will need 5–6 minutes to defrost and heat through. Set aside and allow to cool for a few minutes.

* Crack the eggs into a large bowl and whisk.

* Crumble the feta into the eggs and add the cooked spinach. Season with pepper and nutmeg, if you fancy it. The feta cheese is rather salty, so adding extra salt isn't necessary, although you might want to add it to taste. Whisk all the ingredients together well.

* Heat the frying pan you used to cook the spinach on a medium heat. Pour the egg mixture back into the pan.

* Allow to cook for around 2 minutes. During this time, run a spatula around the edges to ensure the egg does not stick, and swirl the pan every minute or so to allow any liquid egg to travel to the edges and cook. Make sure the hob is not too hot or the bottom of the frittata will burn. The frittata is ready to turn when there is only a small amount of liquid egg left on the top.

* Turn the frittata over very carefully by placing a large plate over the pan. Make sure you wear oven gloves. Flip the frittata quickly onto the plate and slide it back, cooked-side up, into the pan.

* Cook for a further 2 minutes until the frittata is cooked through. Check this by cutting into the centre with a sharp knife to see if the middle is still runny. If it's not properly set, allow to cook for a further minute and check again.

* Serve immediately or cool and wrap in foil. It will keep for 2 days in the fridge if wrapped well.

SPANISH TORTILLA

Serves: 2 (Vegetarian)

A traditional Spanish tortilla is a thick omelette made with potatoes. This one also packs a punch with onion and red pepper. If you have any slices left over, they're great cold for a packed lunch.

1 tbsp olive oil

1 medium potato, peeled and cut into 1cm dice

1 small onion, peeled and chopped finely

½ red pepper, cut into 1cm dice

6 large eggs

Salt and pepper

* Warm the olive oil in a large non-stick frying pan on a medium heat. Add the cubes of potato, and cook for 10 minutes until browned and softened. Add the onion and pepper and cook for another 10 minutes until softened.

* In a bowl, whisk the eggs well. Season with salt and pepper. Pour the egg mixture into the pan over the potato, onion and red pepper.

* Allow to cook for around 5 minutes on a medium heat. During this time, run a spatula around the edges to ensure the egg does not stick, and swirl the pan every minute or so to allow any liquid egg to travel to the edges and cook. Make sure the hob is not too hot or the bottom of the tortilla will burn. The tortilla is ready to turn when there is only a small amount of liquid egg left on the top.

* Turn the tortilla over very carefully by placing a large plate over the pan. Make sure you wear oven gloves. Flip the tortilla quickly onto the plate and slide it back, cooked-side up, into the pan.

* Cook for a further 3–5 minutes until the tortilla is cooked through. Check this by cutting into the centre with a sharp knife to see if the middle is still runny. If it's not properly set, allow to cook for a further 2 minutes and check again.

* Serve immediately or cool and wrap in foil. It will keep for 2 days in the fridge if wrapped well.

CHORIZO AND POTATO FRITTATA

Serves: 2–4

This hearty frittata is really big on flavour, and filling enough to eat for dinner. You need a chunky chorizo sausage rather than the thinly sliced ready-to-eat variety. Serve with green veg or salad – try the superfood salad on page 146.

2 tsp sunflower oil

75g raw cooking chorizo, cut into 1cm chunks

200g small waxy potatoes (such as Charlotte variety), cut into 1cm chunks

6 large eggs

Salt and pepper

* Warm 1 teaspoon of the oil in a medium frying pan (roughly 20cm in diameter) over a medium heat. Add the chorizo and potato chunks, and cook for around 15 minutes until the chorizo is cooked through and the potatoes are soft.

* Meanwhile, crack the eggs into a bowl, add a pinch of salt and pepper and whisk well.

* When the chorizo and potatoes are cooked, add another teaspoon of sunflower oil and heat for a minute or two. Then pour in the eggs and swirl them around so they evenly cover the base of the pan.

* Allow to cook for around 5 minutes on a medium heat. During this time, run a spatula around the edges to ensure the egg does not stick, and swirl the pan every minute or so to allow any liquid egg to travel to the edges and cook. Make sure the hob is not too hot or the bottom of the frittata will burn. The frittata is ready to turn when there is only a small amount of liquid egg left on the top.

* Turn the frittata over very carefully by placing a large plate over the pan. Make sure you wear oven gloves. Flip the frittata quickly onto the plate and slide it back, cooked-side up, into the pan.

* Cook for a further 2 minutes until the frittata is cooked through. Check this by cutting into the centre with a sharp knife to see if the middle is still runny. If it's not properly set, allow to cook for a further minute and check again.

* Serve immediately or cool and wrap in foil. It will keep for 2 days in the fridge if wrapped well.

HAM AND CHEDDAR OMELETTE

Serves: 1

There's a reason why ham and cheese is one of the classic flavour combinations for an omelette – because it tastes so good! Great for dinner and also for breakfast.

1 large knob of butter
3 large eggs
25g ham, torn into pieces
25g mature Cheddar, grated
Salt and pepper

* Melt the butter in a small non-stick frying pan on a medium heat.

* Meanwhile, whisk the eggs together in a bowl, add the ham and grated cheese, and season with salt and pepper. Whisk again well.

* Pour the egg mixture into the pan and swirl it around so it evenly covers the base.

* Allow the omelette to cook for around 2 minutes on a medium heat. During this time, run a spatula around the edges to ensure the egg does not stick, and swirl the pan every minute or so to allow any liquid egg to travel to the edges and cook. Make sure the hob is not too hot or the bottom of the omelette will burn. The omelette is ready to turn when there is only a small amount of liquid egg left on the top.

* Turn the omelette over very carefully by placing a large plate over the pan. Make sure you wear oven gloves. Flip the omelette quickly onto the plate and slide it back, cooked-side up, into the pan.

* Cook for a further 2 minutes until the omelette is cooked through. Check this by cutting into the centre of the omelette with a sharp knife to see if the middle is still runny. If it's not properly set, allow to cook for a further minute and check again.

* Serve immediately or cool and wrap in foil. It will keep for 2 days in the fridge if wrapped well.

BACON AND MUSHROOM OMELETTE

Serves: 1

With simple ingredients but hefty flavours, this quick omelette makes a satisfying dinner. Serve with green veg or salad.

1 large knob of butter

2 rashers of bacon, cut into 1cm strips

3–4 small mushrooms, cut into 5mm thick slices

3 large eggs

Salt and pepper

* Melt the butter in a small non-stick frying pan on a medium heat.

* Add the chopped bacon and mushrooms and cook for around 10 minutes on a medium heat until the bacon is lightly browned and the mushrooms are cooked. If any water comes out of the bacon or mushrooms, allow this to cook off.

* Crack the eggs into a bowl and season with salt and pepper. Whisk together well.

* Pour the egg mixture into the pan and swirl it around so it evenly covers the base.

* Allow the omelette to cook for around 2 minutes on a medium heat. During this time, run a spatula around the edges to ensure it does not stick, and swirl the pan every minute or so to allow any liquid egg to travel to the edges and cook. Make sure the hob is not too hot or the bottom of the omelette will burn. The omelette is ready to turn when there is only a small amount of liquid egg left on the top.

* Turn the omelette over very carefully by placing a large plate over the pan. Make sure you wear oven gloves. Flip the omelette quickly onto the plate and slide it back, cooked-side up, into the pan.

* Cook for a further 2 minutes until the omelette is cooked through. Check this by cutting into the centre of the omelette with a sharp knife to see if the middle is still runny. If it's not properly set, allow to cook for a further minute and check again.

* Serve immediately or cool and wrap in foil. It will keep for 2 days in the fridge if wrapped well.

BAKED FISH WITH TOMATOES AND OLIVES

Serves: 2

You don't need any experience of cooking with fish to make this. As long as you buy boned fillets, it is super-easy, and your kitchen will be full of wonderful smells while it's in the oven. Even better, this recipe leaves behind barely any washing-up.

4 small fillets of fish (see Tip)

25g butter

2 garlic cloves,
peeled and sliced thinly

2 tbsp white wine

8–10 cherry tomatoes

2 tbsp pitted black olives
(from a jar or tin is fine)

Tip: You can make this with any type of white fish. It works really well with frozen fish, too. If baking from frozen, add another 10–15 minutes to the cooking time.

* Preheat the oven to 200°C Fan/Gas Mark 7.

* Prepare your fish by making sure you remove any scales if you can see any. Use skinless, boneless fish if you can.

* Take a large roasting tray and a length of foil twice the length of the tray, then lay the foil evenly across it.

* Cut the butter into small pieces and lay these out on the foil.

* Place the fillets of fish onto the butter, followed by the garlic, wine, tomatoes and olives.

* Fold the excess foil over the top and wrap tightly to form a well-sealed parcel.

* Bake in the oven for 20–30 minutes – the cooking time will depend on the thickness of the fish fillets you use. Don't forget to add on extra cooking time if you are using frozen fish (see Tip).

* Serve with green vegetables and bread to mop up the juices.

EASY THAI FISHCAKES

Serves: 2 (makes 6 small fishcakes)

These make a tasty light lunch or supper. If you have a busy day ahead, prepare them in advance and, once they're coated in breadcrumbs, leave them in the fridge until you're ready to cook.

300g any white fish, skinned, boned and chopped very finely

1 tsp fresh lime juice, plus lime wedges to serve

1 tbsp Thai red curry paste

1 spring onion, finely sliced

1 tsp sweet chilli sauce, plus extra to serve

2 tbsp plain flour

1 large egg, beaten

75g dried breadcrumbs

1 tbsp vegetable oil

Noodles or rice, to serve (optional)

* Place the fish into a bowl and add the lime juice, curry paste, spring onion and chilli sauce and stir together well.

* Take a generous tablespoon of this mixture and roll into a ball. If your fish is quite wet, give the balls a good squeeze as you form them, to remove any excess water. Flatten the ball and place on a plate and repeat. You will get around six fishcakes.

* Cover the plate with cling film and refrigerate the fishcakes for at least 2 hours. Leave overnight if time allows.

* After the fishcakes have been chilled, remove them from the fridge. Sprinkle the flour on one plate, put the beaten egg in a shallow bowl and spread the dried breadcrumbs on another plate. Take one fishcake at a time and coat first in flour, then egg and then breadcrumbs in that order. Repeat with the remaining fishcakes.

* In a large frying pan, warm the oil over a medium heat.

* Cook the fishcakes until they are golden, which will take roughly 4–5 minutes on each side. Try not to move the fishcakes too much when they are cooking as they will be quite soft.

* Once cooked, serve immediately, with a lime wedge and some extra sweet chilli sauce for dipping. For a more substantial dish, serve with noodles or rice.

STORE-CUPBOARD SALMON FISHCAKES

Serves: 2 (makes 4 large fishcakes)

Stock your cupboard with a few key ingredients and you can rustle up these delicious fishcakes whenever you're running low on fresh supplies. If you feel like jazzing these up, add a tablespoon of capers, chopped parsley or coriander, or some thinly sliced spring onions to the mixture before cooking.

350g large floury potatoes, peeled and cut into halves

215g can salmon, well drained

1 tbsp mayonnaise, plus extra to serve

1 tbsp capers, chopped parsley or coriander, or sliced spring onions (optional)

3 tbsp plain flour

1 egg, beaten

75g dried breadcrumbs

2–3 tbsp sunflower oil

Salt and pepper

Lemon wedges, to serve

Tip: The uncooked fishcakes can be frozen individually (take care not to squash them!) and then pan-fried once defrosted.

* Boil the potatoes for around 15–20 minutes until cooked. Drain well, then mash them and set them aside to cool slightly.

* Place the salmon in a mixing bowl and flake the fish using a fork to break it up. Ensure any skin or bones are removed from the bowl before moving on to the next step.

* Add the cooled mashed potato to the bowl, followed by the mayonnaise and a generous pinch of salt and pepper and mix to combine all the ingredients evenly. If you wish to add capers, parsley or coriander or spring onions, now is the time.

* Sprinkle the flour on one plate, put the beaten egg in a shallow bowl and spread the dried breadcrumbs on another plate.

* Divide the fishcake mixture into four and roll into balls roughly the size of tennis balls.

* Flatten each ball with your hands and then coat first in flour, then egg and then breadcrumbs in that order. Repeat with the remaining fishcakes.

* In a large frying pan, warm the oil over a medium heat.

* Cook the fishcakes until they are golden, which will take roughly 4–5 minutes on each side. Try not to move the fishcakes too much when they are cooking as they will be quite soft.

* Once cooked, serve immediately with salad or vegetables, and possibly a lemon wedge and another dollop of mayonnaise.

LAMB MEATBALLS WITH COUSCOUS

Serves: 4

These slightly spicy meatballs are cooked in a rich tomato sauce. Lamb can often be quite pricy but buying it as mince means you can enjoy it without breaking the bank.

For the meatballs

350g lamb mince

1 red onion, peeled and chopped finely

2 garlic cloves, peeled and chopped finely

3 tsp ground cumin

2 tsp ground cinnamon

Pinch of hot chilli powder

1 tbsp olive oil

2 x 400g cans chopped tomatoes

300ml hot chicken stock

1 tsp caster sugar

2 tbsp tomato purée

Salt and pepper

For the couscous

1 red and 1 yellow pepper, deseeded and chopped into 2cm chunks

1 courgette, cut into 1cm thick slices

1 red onion, peeled and cut into 8 pieces

2 tbsp olive oil

300g couscous

350ml hot chicken stock

Salt and pepper

* Preheat the oven to 180°C Fan/Gas Mark 6.

* Place the mince, half the chopped onion and half the chopped garlic in a large bowl. Add the cumin, cinnamon, chilli powder and salt and pepper and mix everything together well. Pinch off walnut-sized pieces of the mixture and roll into balls.

* Heat the olive oil in a large frying pan and add the meatballs. Cook for 10–15 minutes on a medium-high heat until the meatballs are well browned all over. Remove from the pan and set aside.

* Add the remaining onion and garlic to the pan and cook for a couple of minutes until softened and fragrant.

* Add the canned tomatoes, stock, sugar and tomato purée and stir well. Leave to bubble away, covered with a lid, for 10 minutes.

* Meanwhile, place the peppers, courgette and red onion in a large roasting tray. Pour over 1 tablespoon of the olive oil. Toss the vegetables well in the oil until lightly coated.

* Transfer the meatballs and the sauce from the frying pan to a large ovenproof baking dish. Cover with a lid or foil and place in the oven along with the vegetables on another shelf. Bake both dishes for 30 minutes.

* After 25 minutes, place the couscous into a large bowl. Pour over the hot chicken stock. Cover the bowl with cling film and leave for 5 minutes.

* Take the cling film off the couscous and fluff it up using a fork to separate the grains. Season with salt and pepper. Remove the vegetables from the oven and stir them through the couscous. You may wish to add another glug of olive oil.

* Serve the couscous with the meatballs and warm pitta bread.

QUICK SWEET-AND-SOUR PORK

Serves: 4

This fast, super-easy dish tastes just as good as the takeaway version!

1 tsp olive oil

2 garlic cloves,
peeled and crushed

3cm piece of fresh root ginger,
peeled and finely grated

500g pork loin,
sliced into 2cm cubes

1 small can pineapple rings
in juice, drained and cut into
2.5cm chunks

1 red pepper, deseeded and
chopped into 2.5cm chunks

3 tbsp soy sauce

3 tbsp tomato ketchup

1–2 tsp honey

* Heat the oil in a large frying pan and cook the garlic and ginger over a medium heat until they start to soften slightly. Don't let them brown.

* Add the pork and cook until it is lightly browned. This should take around 10 minutes.

* Add the remaining ingredients, using more or less honey depending on your taste. Stir together well and cook for another 10 minutes or so until the pork is cooked through.

* Serve on a bed of steamed rice or with egg fried rice (page 161).

CREAMY HONEY AND MUSTARD PORK CHOPS

Serves: 2

In just half an hour, and with only a little chopping and stirring, you can serve up a delicious dinner that will impress everyone who tries it.

20g butter

2 pork chops

½ large onion, peeled and sliced

2 eating apples, peeled, cored and sliced

1 tsp runny honey

1 tbsp wholegrain mustard

150ml good-quality cider

4 tbsp double cream

Mashed potato and vegetables, to serve

* Over a medium heat, melt the butter in a large frying pan.

* Add the pork chops and allow to brown on both sides. This should take 3–4 minutes each side.

* Add the onion to the pan and allow it to soften for around 5 minutes.

* Add the apple, honey, mustard, cider and cream, stir well and allow to bubble away for around 10–15 minutes.

* Serve the pork chops with mashed potato and vegetables and plenty of the sauce spooned on top.

HAM AND CHEESE EMPANADAS

Makes: 8 small empanadas

An empanada is a delicious savoury stuffed pastry. These cheese and ham ones are seriously addictive, simple to make and very transportable. Any leftovers make a perfect packed lunch.

375g packet of
ready-rolled puff pastry

60g ham, chopped
into 1cm squares

70g mature Cheddar, grated

1 egg, beaten

* Preheat the oven to 200°C Fan/Gas Mark 7.

* Line a baking sheet with non-stick baking paper and set aside.

* Use a large mug, glass or cookie cutter to cut out circles of pastry – about 10cm in diameter is ideal. Repeat until all the pastry has been used up. Transfer the circles of pastry to the prepared baking sheet.

* Place a few squares of ham and a little cheese in the centre of each disc of pastry. Brush the edges with beaten egg. If you don't have a pastry brush, just dab with your fingers. Fold the pastry over to form a half-moon shape.

* With a fork, press down the edges of each empanada to seal it so that the cheese does not bubble out when it cooks.

* Make two small cuts on the top of each empanada using a sharp knife to let steam escape while cooking.

* Brush or dab the top of the empanandas with more beaten egg.

* Transfer to the oven and bake for 15 minutes until golden brown. Eat immediately (though any leftovers are delicious cold too). To store leftovers, allow to cool thoroughly, wrap in foil and keep in the fridge for up to 2 days.

BAKED SAUSAGES WITH APPLES AND CIDER

Serves: 4

A bit of booze turns bangers into a simple but special supper. Make sure you use a decent-quality cider, either sweet or dry, but not super-strength or anything flavoured.

2 tbsp olive oil

20g butter

8–12 large pork sausages
(2–3 per person, depending
on appetite)

1 garlic clove,
peeled and chopped

1 large onion, peeled and
chopped into 8 wedges

3 eating apples,
cored and cut in half

2 bay leaves

2 tsp dried thyme or 2 large
sprigs of fresh thyme

250ml cider

Mashed potato or bread,
to serve

* Preheat the oven to 200°C Fan/Gas Mark 7.

* Warm the olive oil and butter in a large frying pan over a medium heat. Add the sausages, garlic and onion, and cook for 10 minutes or so until the sausages have started to brown and the onion is lightly browned too.

* Tip the contents of the pan into a large ovenproof baking dish. Add the apple, bay leaves and thyme to the dish and bake for 30 minutes.

* After this time, remove the dish from the oven and give everything a good stir. Pour the cider into the dish and return to the oven.

* Bake for a further 30 minutes. Once cooked, the sausages should be really browned and the onion and apple should be very soft and browned.

* Serve with mashed potato, and/or fresh bread to mop up the juices.

Tip: Buy the best-quality sausages you can afford. It will make this dish taste even better.

FIFTEEN-MINUTE BURGER
AND HOMEMADE CHIPS

Serves: 1

Try this burger and chips for an easy treat. The burger really benefits from being made with the best-quality beef and cheese you can afford. If you like, you can serve it in a bun with mayo and red onion.

1 medium potato

1 tbsp grated mature Cheddar or Parmesan

125g minced steak

Sunflower oil

Salt and pepper

Burger bun, to serve (optional)

* Boil the kettle, then pour the boiling water into a large saucepan and place over a high heat.

* Cut the potato into 5mm-wide sticks and plunge them into the boiling water. Boil for 3 minutes, drain and pat dry with kitchen paper or a clean tea towel.

* Grate the cheese into a bowl, add the mince and season with salt and pepper. Mix together with your hands. Shape into a ball and flatten slightly.

* In a non-stick frying pan, heat 1 tablespoon of the oil over a medium to high heat. Place the burger into the frying pan and cook for around 3–4 minutes on one side.

* Check on the burger by lifting it up with a fish slice or metal spatula. If it is browned on the underside, flip it over. Cook for 3–4 minutes on the other side, until browned and juicy but still pink inside when cut open. Leave to keep warm in the pan.

* Meanwhile, in another large frying pan add enough oil to cover the base and heat over a medium to high heat. Add the sticks of potato and fry. Turn the potatoes over every minute or so, to make sure they are evenly cooked.

* When the potatoes are crisp and brown, remove and drain on kitchen paper. Serve the burger and chips on their own, or with a tomato and lettuce salad. If you're hungry, pop the burger in a bun.

MOZZARELLA AND PESTO-STUFFED CHICKEN BREASTS

Serves: 2

This recipe involves just a few minutes of prep, then you can simply bang it in the oven and a delicious dinner will soon be waiting for you.

2 boneless, skinless chicken breasts

6 tsp basil pesto

125g ball of mozzarella, cut into 4 thick slices

Salt and pepper

* Preheat the oven to 180°C Fan/Gas Mark 6. Cut a deep slit down the top of each chicken fillet. Insert 2 teaspoons of pesto and place a slice of mozzarella inside each slit.

* Put the stuffed chicken breasts in an ovenproof baking dish. Make sure it has sides as the chicken will release lots of juices as it cooks. Spread another teaspoon of pesto on top of each chicken breast and top with a final slice of mozzarella. Season with salt and pepper.

* Bake for 20–30 minutes, depending on the size of the chicken breasts. The mozzarella should be golden and bubbling. Cut the chicken open to check the meat is no longer pink before serving. If the meat is still slightly pink, return it to the oven for a further 5 minutes and then test again.

THAI CHICKEN DRUMSTICKS

Serves: 2

These yummy spicy drumsticks need to be left for a few hours to absorb all the Thai flavours before cooking. Enjoy hot or cold.

4–6 chicken drumsticks

4 tsp Thai red curry paste

Grated zest and juice of 1 lime

3cm piece of fresh root ginger, peeled and grated

* Place the chicken drumsticks into a large bowl.

* Add the curry paste, lime zest and juice, and ginger. Stir together well, cover with cling film and refrigerate for several hours or overnight.

* When you are ready to cook the drumsticks, preheat the oven to 200°C Fan/Gas Mark 7.

* Lay the drumsticks out in a large roasting tray and bake for 30–40 minutes until the chicken is cooked through and the skin is crisp. Serve with rice or salad.

HEALTHY 'FRIED' CHICKEN

Serves: 4

If fried chicken is one of your guilty pleasures, here's a great way to make it a bit *less* guilty! There's actually no frying involved; instead this recipe uses the oven, which means it's easier to cook and is a bit better for you without all that oil. Buttermilk can be found in supermarkets near the milk and cream.

**4 chicken legs or roughly
900g chicken pieces,
skin on or removed,
whichever you prefer**

284ml carton of buttermilk

100g dried breadcrumbs

Salt and pepper

Oven chips, to serve (optional)

* Place the chicken into a large plastic food bag. Pour in the buttermilk and season with salt and pepper.

* Tie a knot in the top of the bag or seal with a clip and rub the chicken and buttermilk together through the bag. Place into the fridge for an hour or even overnight to let the flavour intensify.

* When you are ready to cook the chicken, preheat the oven to 180°C Fan/Gas Mark 6.

* Place the breadcrumbs onto a plate and roll the chicken pieces one by one in the breadcrumbs to coat them thoroughly, then lay them out in a roasting tray.

* Once all the pieces of chicken have been crumbed, bake them in the oven for 20 minutes. Remove from the oven, turn the pieces of chicken over and bake for a further 20–25 minutes until the chicken is cooked through.

* Serve with oven chips, salad or coleslaw, as you like.

BUTTERNUT SQUASH RISOTTO

Serves: 4 (Vegetarian)

This tasty, wallet-friendly risotto is baked in the oven, making it much easier than a traditional risotto, which involves constant stirring on the hob. Make sure you use risotto rice, as other varieties don't work in the same way (see Tip, page 109).

2 tbsp olive oil

600g butternut squash, peeled, seeds removed and cut into 1cm dice

30g butter

1 large onion, peeled and finely chopped

2 garlic cloves, peeled and chopped

275g arborio risotto rice

875ml hot vegetable or chicken stock

65g Parmesan (or vegetarian equivalent), finely grated

Salt and pepper

* Preheat the oven to 180°C Fan/Gas mark 6.

* Pour the olive oil into a large roasting tray. Add the butternut squash cubes and toss well to ensure each cube is covered in oil. Set aside.

* Melt the butter in a large saucepan. Add the onion and garlic and cook for a couple of minutes over a medium heat until softened and fragrant.

* Add the risotto rice and stir through well.

* Add the hot stock and season with salt and pepper. You may want to go easy on the salt as stock cubes are already salty.

* Bring the risotto to the boil. When it starts to bubble, carefully transfer the contents of the pan to a large ovenproof baking dish.

* Bake the dish of risotto and tray of butternut squash separately in the oven for 12 minutes.

* After this time, stir the risotto, cover the dish with foil and bake both the rice and squash for another 8–10 minutes until the rice is tender.

* Scatter the cubes of squash over the risotto, sprinkle with Parmesan and serve immediately.

LEMON RISOTTO

Serves: 4 (Vegetarian)

This fresh and summery risotto calls for just a few simple ingredients. Baking risotto in the oven is much easier than making it the traditional way on the hob as you don't have to stand and stir it continuously. Make sure you use risotto rice, as other varieties don't work in the same way (see Tip).

30g butter

1 large onion,
peeled and finely chopped

2 garlic cloves,
peeled and chopped

Grated zest and juice
of ½ lemon

275g arborio risotto rice

875ml hot vegetable or
chicken stock

65g Parmesan (or vegetarian
equivalent), finely grated

Salt and pepper

* Preheat the oven to 180°C Fan/Gas mark 6.

* Melt the butter in a large saucepan. Add the onion and garlic and cook for a couple of minutes over a medium heat until softened and fragrant.

* Now add the lemon juice and zest and risotto rice and stir through well.

* Add the hot stock and season with salt and pepper. You may want to go easy on the salt as stock cubes are already salty.

* Bring the risotto to the boil. When it starts to bubble, carefully transfer the contents of the pan to a large ovenproof baking dish.

* Bake the risotto for 12 minutes in the oven.

* After this time, stir the risotto, cover the dish with foil and bake for another 8–10 minutes until the rice is tender.

* Sprinkle with Parmesan and serve immediately.

Tip: You need risotto rice, such as arborio, to get the best result. This type of short-grain rice has lots of floury starch, which is what makes the risotto thick and creamy.

CHEESY BAKED AUBERGINES

Serves: 4 (Vegetarian)

This is a delicious dish of aubergines layered with tomato sauce and mozarella. It's a great vegetarian alternative to lasagne. If you have any leftovers, they can easily be reheated in the microwave.

5 tsp olive oil

3 medium aubergines, sliced lengthways into large slices, about 1.5cm thick

2 garlic cloves, peeled and finely chopped

2 x 400g cans chopped tomatoes

Pinch of caster sugar

1 tsp dried basil or 1 tbsp chopped fresh basil

250g mozzarella, cut into 1cm slices

50g Parmesan (or vegetarian equivalent) or other strongly flavoured hard cheese, finely grated

Salt and pepper

* Preheat the oven to 180°C Fan/Gas Mark 6.

* Grease two baking sheets each with 2 teaspoons of the olive oil. Lay the aubergine slices on the baking sheet and put in the oven for 15–20 minutes, until soft and turning golden brown.

* Warm the remaining teaspoon of olive oil into a saucepan, add the garlic and cook over a gentle heat for 2–3 minutes.

* Meanwhile, drain the juice out of the cans of tomatoes and add the tomato flesh to the garlic in the saucepan. Stir and leave to bubble away for 10–15 minutes, covered with a lid, stirring occasionally.

* When the aubergine slices are baked, take them out of the oven, season with salt and pepper and then arrange a layer of aubergine slices in the bottom of a medium-sized ovenproof baking dish. Leave the oven turned on.

* Season the tomato sauce with the salt, pepper and sugar, and add the basil. Stir well and then top the layer of aubergines with a layer of tomato sauce and a few slices of mozzarella.

* Repeat the layers until all of the aubergine, tomato sauce and mozzarella has been used, finishing with a final layer of aubergine. If you are using a large dish, you may only have enough ingredients for two layers, so put all the sauce and mozzarella on top of the first layer of aubergine and then top with a second layer of aubergines.

* Sprinkle the dish with the Parmesan or hard cheese and bake for 20–25 minutes until it is golden and bubbling. Leave for 10 minutes before cutting into portions and serving.

FEEDING FRIENDS

SPICY NUTS

Serves: 3–4 (Vegetarian)

These spicy nuts are a perfect snack for movie nights or to nibble with drinks. They are totally moreish and will fill your mouth with spicy, salty and sweet flavours all at the same time.

200g plain mixed nuts
60g butter
4 tbsp dark brown soft sugar
½ tsp chilli flakes
½ tsp cayenne pepper
½ tsp sea salt

* Place the nuts in a large, dry, non-stick frying pan over a medium heat. You want to toast the nuts, so cook for around 4–5 minutes, shaking the pan occasionally. The nuts may brown a little.

* Once the nuts are toasted, add the butter, sugar, chilli, cayenne and sea salt to the pan.

* Stir everything together to ensure the nuts are well coated. When the coating starts to bubble in the bottom of the pan, give everything a final stir and tip out onto a sheet of baking paper. Make sure the nuts are well spread out and not clumped together.

* Leave to cool for at least 5 minutes before serving, which will allow the coating to solidify.

* Tip into a bowl, not missing any of the lovely sugary bits, and enjoy while still warm.

TZATZIKI

Serves: 4 (Vegetarian)

This yoghurt and cucumber dip is a doddle to make. It's gorgeous served with carrot sticks or tortilla chips, or in a pitta with falafel.

½ cucumber, grated
1 tsp salt
120g natural yoghurt
1 tbsp olive oil
½ small garlic clove, peeled and crushed

* Put the grated cucumber into a sieve placed over a bowl. Sprinkle over the salt and leave for 15 minutes.

* In handfuls, pick up the cucumber and, over the sink, squeeze as much water as you can out of it. Place the cucumber back in the sieve and leave for another 15 minutes. Don't skip this step, otherwise your dip will be too runny!

* Give the cucumber another squeeze and place it into a clean bowl. Spoon in the yoghurt, oil and garlic and stir together well.

* Serve straight away – this dip doesn't keep.

HOMEMADE HOUMOUS

Serves: 4–6 (Vegetarian)

Everyone loves houmous, and although it's easy to pick up a tub from the supermarket, it's much cheaper and tastier to make your own – and your mates will be impressed. To achieve a really smooth, silky houmous, you need a blender or food processor, but for a rough-textured houmous, a potato masher works just fine.

2 x 400g cans chickpeas, drained

2 tbsp lemon juice

2 small garlic cloves, peeled and finely chopped

2 tsp tahini paste

60ml good-quality olive oil

Salt and pepper

* Place all the ingredients into a food processor or blender and blitz for a minute or two until you have a smooth purée.

* Serve with crisps, breadsticks, toasted pitta bread or raw vegetable sticks to dip in, with an extra drizzle of olive oil on the top, if desired.

* This houmous will keep for 5 days in the fridge in a well-sealed plastic container.

Tip: If you prefer your houmous with a stronger flavour, add a little more garlic and lemon juice.

LOADED NACHOS

Serves: 4 (Vegetarian)

Preparing nachos at home costs a fraction of the price of buying them in a bar or restaurant. They are perfect party food, heaped high with all your favourite toppings, such as melted cheese, salsa, soured cream and whatever else you want to throw on there. Definitely nicest eaten warm.

1 large packet of plain tortilla chips

200g cheese (Cheddar, Monterey Jack or similar), grated

Add extras to your taste

Leftover chilli (page 61 or vegetarian), reheated in the microwave or in a saucepan

Jalapeño pepper slices

Guacamole

Soured cream

Salsa

* Preheat the grill to a medium–high heat.

* Spread the tortilla chips evenly over the base of a large baking dish and sprinkle the cheese over them. If you are using chilli con carne, spoon the hot sauce in blobs on top of the cheese.

* Put the dish under the grill for around 3–4 minutes until the cheese has melted.

* Top the hot nachos with a scattering of jalapeños and spoonfuls of guacamole, soured cream and salsa, dotted around the dish evenly. Use as much or as little of each ingredient as you like – everyone has different tastes – but add at least 2 tablespoons of each.

* Serve and enjoy immediately.

STUFFED POTATO SKINS

Serves: 4 (Vegetarian)

These cheesy treats are crispy on the outside and fluffy on the inside! Great as part of a meal, they also make a very satisfying snack and very much fall into the comfort food category.

4 baking potatoes
(check the variety you buy
is suitable for baking)

140g mature Cheddar, grated

100ml soured cream (optional)

2 spring onions, thinly sliced

Salt and pepper

* Preheat the oven to 220°C Fan/Gas Mark 9.

* Use a sharp knife to prick your potatoes well five or six times all over. This will prevent them from potentially exploding in the oven.

* Wash your potatoes well and shake off the excess water. While the potato skins are still slightly damp, sprinkle salt over each potato and rub it all over the skin.

* Bake the potatoes directly on the oven shelf for around 50–75 minutes, depending on the size of your potatoes.

* Test if the potatoes are done by sticking a sharp knife into them to see how soft they feel. When cooked enough, the knife should easily slip into the potatoes. The skin should also feel crisp to the touch. If they're not quite cooked, bake for a further 10 minutes and test again.

* Once the potatoes are cooked, cut in half and scoop out the flesh from the skin. Place the fluffy potato into a bowl. Add 50g of the cheese, the soured cream and spring onion, season with salt and pepper and mix well.

* Spoon the potato mixture back into the skins. Sprinkle the remaining cheese on top.

* Bake the skins again for 20 minutes until golden and the cheese has melted.

BLACK BEAN QUESADILLAS

Serves: 2–4 (Vegetarian)

If you've never tried a quesadilla, they are something like a Mexican version of a toastie. They're quick and easy to rustle up and great for friends as they can be made in large quantities and always please a crowd. Feel free to vary the fillings and toppings as you fancy.

400g canned black beans, drained and rinsed

2 spring onions, sliced finely

1 pepper, chopped finely

80g mature Cheddar, grated

½ tsp ground cumin

½ tsp dried oregano

Finely grated zest of 1 lime, plus wedges to serve

4 large tortilla wraps

Chilli sauce, to serve

Tip: If you want to have a go at making the tortillas yourself, see page 121. Otherwise, bought ones are fine.

* Place the black beans, spring onions, chopped pepper, grated cheese, cumin, oregano and lime zest into a bowl and lightly mash together using a fork or potato masher. You don't want it to be a purée, just crush the beans slightly and mix the ingredients together.

* Lay one tortilla on a board. Spoon the bean mixture onto the tortilla and, using the back of a spoon, spread it evenly over the tortilla, to about 2cm from the edge.

* Place the second tortilla on top of the bean mixture and press down to form a kind of tortilla sandwich.

* Place a large non-stick frying pan on a medium–high heat.

* Transfer the filled tortillas into the dry frying pan. Note that you do not need to use oil to cook this.

* After about 1½ minutes you should notice the tortilla browning. Flip it over and cook the other side.

* The quesadilla is ready to serve when the cheese is melted inside and the tortillas are brown on both sides.

* Cut the quesadilla up into quarters and pile them up on a plate. Enjoy immediately, served with lime wedges and chilli sauce.

PATATAS BRAVAS

Serves: 2–4 (Vegetarian)

Patatas bravas are bite-sized roasted potatoes topped with a spicy tomato sauce. If you've ever been to Spain, you'll know they are served everywhere. They are great to share with friends over a drink or while watching a film, and will disappear in a flash at a party or barbecue.

6 tbsp olive oil

500g waxy potatoes (such as Charlotte variety), peeled and chopped into 2cm chunks

1 red onion, peeled and finely chopped

1 garlic clove, peeled and chopped

400g can chopped tomatoes

Generous pinch of sugar

½ tsp chilli powder

Salt and pepper

* Preheat the oven to 200°C Fan/Gas mark 7.

* Place 4 tablespoons of the oil into a large ovenproof roasting tray or baking tin and heat in the oven for 3 minutes.

* Remove the tray from the oven and place the potato chunks in it. Stir them around to ensure each chunk is coated in oil. Bake for 35–45 minutes until browned and crispy.

* Meanwhile, make the tomato sauce. Warm the remaining 2 tablespoons of olive oil in a saucepan. Add the onion and garlic and cook for 5 minutes over a medium heat so that they soften.

* Add the can of tomatoes, sugar and chilli powder and season with salt and pepper. While the potatoes are roasting, allow the sauce to bubble away for 20–30 minutes until thickened.

* Once the potatoes are roasted, spread the tomato sauce on a large plate.

* Place the potatoes on top of the sauce so that they stay crisp. Season with extra salt and pepper if desired. Serve immediately.

CHICKEN FAJITAS

Serves: 4

Fajitas are perfect sharing food and doing them yourself is cheaper than buying a fajita 'kit'. Once you've fried the meat and veg, simply lay everything out in bowls and let everyone build their own meal.

3 boneless, skinless chicken breasts, sliced into 1cm strips

2 tsp paprika

½ tsp ground cumin

Grated zest and juice of 3 limes

1 tsp olive oil

1 red pepper, deseeded and cut into 1cm strips

1 green pepper, deseeded and cut into 1cm strips

1 large red onion, peeled and thinly sliced

4 tortillas, shop-bought or homemade, to serve

Guacamole, sour cream, grated Cheddar cheese or salsa (optional toppings)

* Place the sliced chicken, paprika, cumin, lime zest and juice into a bowl. Stir together well, cover with cling film and leave to marinate for at least an hour.

* Meanwhile, make sure you have the tortillas and fillings ready.

* Warm the oil in a frying pan over a high heat. Tip in the chicken and any marinade. Add the peppers and onion and fry, keeping the heat high, for around 10–15 minutes until the chicken is cooked through and the vegetables are softened. See if the chicken is cooked through by cutting up a larger piece and checking there is no pink meat left inside.

* Serve the chicken immediately on a tortilla, with your favourite toppings, such as guacamole, sour cream, grated Cheddar cheese and salsa. Roll up and eat straight away!

HOMEMADE TORTILLAS

Serves: 4 (Vegetarian)

Use these simple tortillas as wraps, or in recipes like the fajitas above.

120g self-raising flour

1½ tsp vegetable or sunflower oil

60ml warm water

Pinch of salt

* Place the flour in a bowl and add the oil, water and salt. Mix well to form a stiff dough.

* Divide the mixture into four balls. Place one ball of mixture at a time out onto a clean, floured work surface. Roll into a thin circle.

* Heat a large, dry non-stick frying pan over a high heat. When the pan is really hot, place a tortilla into the pan and cook for 30–50 seconds on each side. Flip the tortilla when it is just lightly brown. Repeat.

STICKY BAKED CHINESE CHICKEN LEGS

Serves: 4

Chicken legs tend to be fairly cheap, and it can be good value to buy a big packet and freeze any extras. You may need to buy the five-spice and star anise specially for this recipe, but they do make all the difference and once you've got them in the cupboard it's a good excuse to make this delicious recipe again and again!

3 garlic cloves, peeled and sliced finely

3cm piece of fresh root ginger, peeled and sliced finely

120ml soy sauce

4 tsp honey

4 star anise

2 tsp Chinese five-spice powder

4 chicken legs, skin on

Rice, to serve

* Place all the ingredients except the chicken together in a bowl and stir well to combine.

* Add the chicken legs and stir to cover in the sauce. Cover the bowl with cling film and let it sit in the fridge for several hours or overnight.

* When you are ready to cook the chicken, preheat the oven to 200°C Fan/Gas Mark 7.

* Place the chicken pieces and the sauce into an ovenproof baking dish. Bake for 30–35 minutes until the chicken is no longer pink when cut open and the skin is crisp.

* Serve with rice and any extra sauce drizzled on top. Garnish with the star anise if you like.

CHICKEN, BACON AND LEEK PIE

Serves: 4–6

A homemade pie is pure comfort food and this is no exception, with a rich filling and lots of flaky pastry. If you've never made a pie before, don't be nervous – this one is quick, fuss-free and uses ready-made pastry. If you're feeding lots of people, make the pie go further by serving with a big mound of mashed potato.

55g butter

3 leeks, washed and sliced into 1cm thick rings

4 rashers of smoked back bacon, cut into 1cm strips

300g cooked chicken (you can use leftover roast chicken)

40g plain flour

400ml hot chicken stock

1 bay leaf

1 tsp dried thyme

375g packet of ready-made puff pastry

1 large egg, beaten

Salt and pepper

Mashed potato, to serve

Tip: Don't worry if you don't have a rolling pin – a clean wine bottle will do the job perfectly well!

* Preheat the oven to 200°C Fan/Gas Mark 7.

* Melt the butter over a gentle heat in a large frying pan. Add the leek rings and strips of bacon. Cook for around 10–15 minutes until the leek is softened and the bacon is cooked. Don't allow the leek to colour. It may seem as though there is a lot of butter, but don't worry.

* Add the cooked chicken and flour and stir to incorporate all the ingredients evenly.

* Pour the hot stock into the pan. Add the bay leaf and thyme and season with salt and pepper (you may not want to use much salt as stock is already salty). Stir well and allow to bubble away gently for 10 minutes.

* Meanwhile, prepare the pastry. Place a large sheet of cling film out on the work surface, put the block of pastry on top and cover with a second sheet of cling film. Roll the pastry out between the two sheets until it is large enough to cover the top of a shallow ovenproof baking dish or pie dish. The pastry should fit right up to the edges of the dish.

* Transfer the pie filling from the pan into the oven dish. Lay the pastry over the top. If you have any excess pastry, just tuck it down the sides of the dish. Cut a cross in the top of the pastry to allow any steam to escape while cooking.

* Brush the pastry with the beaten egg to glaze so that it will turn a lovely colour when baking. If you do not have a pastry brush, just dab with your fingers.

* Bake the pie for 20–25 minutes until the pastry is puffed up and golden brown. The filling should be piping hot.

* Serve with vegetables and mashed potato.

SLOW-COOKED PORK

Serves: 4 generously

This delicious pork joint is totally worth the time it takes to cook, and it takes no time at all to prepare – just mix up the sauce, rub it onto the meat and bang it in the oven. The long stint in the oven makes the pork so tender that it will fall apart into shreds once cooked. Any leftovers are great in sandwiches.

1kg joint of pork shoulder

1 tbsp sunflower oil

2 large onions, peeled and chopped

6 garlic cloves, peeled and chopped

1 tsp hot chilli powder

1 tsp black pepper

4 tbsp tomato ketchup

2 tsp cider vinegar

2 tsp Worcestershire or barbecue sauce

Mashed potato, to serve

* Preheat the oven to 170°C Fan/Gas Mark 5.

* Place the joint of pork in a large ovenproof baking dish. If the joint is tied with string, leave it on until the meat is cooked.

* In a separate bowl combine the oil, onion, garlic, chilli powder, black pepper, ketchup, cider vinegar and Worcestershire or barbecue sauce. Stir well to form a thick sauce.

* Tip the sauce into the ovenproof dish and rub it all over the pork joint.

* Cover the dish with a lid or tin foil and bake in the oven for 3 hours, giving the sauce a good stir every 45 minutes or so to ensure it doesn't burn.

* When the meat is cooked it will start to fall apart. Remove the pork from the baking dish, cut off the string (if there is any) and peel off the fat.

* Now you can simply pull the pork apart using two forks and serve immediately with mashed potato and vegetables. The sauce in the bottom of the dish makes a delicious accompaniment to the meat.

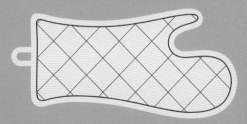

HALLOUMI AND ROASTED VEGETABLES WITH LEMON DRESSING

Serves: 4 (Vegetarian)

This light meal is lovely in summer and ideal for serving to your vegetarian friends. Halloumi is a firm cheese that can be fried or grilled and still holds its shape. It has quite a salty flavour, so the lemony dressing is a nice contrast here.

5 tbsp olive oil

1 red pepper, deseeded and cut into 2cm chunks

2 courgettes, cut into 1cm slices

1 aubergine, cut into 2cm cubes

3 medium tomatoes, cut into quarters

1 red onion, peeled and cut into 6 wedges

1 tbsp plain flour

1 halloumi cheese (approximately 225–250g), cut lengthways into 1cm slices

For the dressing

Juice of ½ lemon

1 tsp capers

Fresh coriander (optional)

Salt and pepper

* Preheat the oven to 180°C Fan/Gas Mark 6.

* Pour 2 tablespoons of the olive oil into a large roasting tray. Place the pepper, courgette, aubergine, tomato and onion into the roasting tray, spread out evenly and place in the oven to roast for 25–30 minutes until the vegetables are browned and soft.

* Meanwhile, sprinkle the flour on a plate and season well with salt and pepper. Take the slices of halloumi and cover them with flour on both sides.

* Heat 1 tablespoon of the oil in a small frying pan on a medium temperature for a minute or so. Then place the floured slices of halloumi into the pan.

* Fry the halloumi for 1 minute on each side until it is golden brown and feels soft.

* Make the lemon dressing by whisking the remaining 2 tablespoons of olive oil with the lemon juice, capers, salt and pepper and fresh coriander, if you are using.

* Serve the roasted vegetables with the halloumi. Pour the lemon dressing over the top to serve.

HOMEMADE PIZZA

Makes: 1 large pizza (Vegetarian)

You can't beat a homemade pizza. It's infinitely tastier and cheaper than a takeaway or frozen one from the supermarket. If you're cooking for a crowd, simply multiply the recipe accordingly.

200g strong white bread flour

½ tsp salt

⅓ tsp fast-action dried yeast

¼ tsp sugar

125ml warm water

2 tsp olive oil

Toppings of choice
(see suggestion below)

Tip: Pizza dough freezes very well, so you can make extra, freeze the dough once shaped and then defrost and bake another time.

* Sift the flour and salt through a sieve into a large mixing bowl and add the yeast and sugar. Add the warm water (it should be body temperature) and 1 teaspoon of the oil and mix until the mixture comes together to make a sticky dough.

* Turn the dough out onto a floured work surface and knead gently for a couple of minutes until the dough starts to feel smoother.

* Place the dough back into the bowl, cover with cling film and a clean tea towel and leave in a warm place to rise for an hour. This can be near a warm oven or in the sunlight near a window. The dough should almost double in size.

* Preheat the oven to 220°C Fan/Gas Mark 9. Grease a large baking sheet lightly with the remaining 1 teaspoon of oil.

* Turn the dough out onto a lightly floured surface again and knead gently for around 5 minutes until it feels smooth, less sticky and elastic. Shape the dough into a circle as thick or thin as you like.

* Transfer the dough to the baking sheet and add your favourite toppings (see suggestion below). Bake for 10 minutes, then slide the pizza off the baking sheet onto the oven shelf and bake for another 2–3 minutes until the base is golden and crispy and the toppings are melted.

* Serve immediately. Any leftovers are great for a packed lunch.

MARGHERITA PIZZA

For a delicious tomato sauce to top your pizza, warm 2 teaspoons of olive oil in a small saucepan on a medium heat. Add 2 peeled, chopped garlic cloves and cook for 2 minutes until fragrant. Add a 400g can of chopped tomatoes and season with salt, pepper and 1 teaspoon caster sugar. Cook for around 15 minutes until thickened. Cool and spread over your pizza base. Top with 60g mozzarella cheese, torn into strips, and add any other toppings you like.

TOAD IN THE HOLE WITH ONION GRAVY

Serves: 4

Great as an alternative Sunday lunch, toad in the hole is a real crowd-pleaser. You can add extra sausages if you're feeding big appetites, and use any type you fancy – if you like flavoured ones, go for it. This also works with vegetarian sausages if you don't eat meat.

For the toad in the hole

300ml full-fat milk

2 large eggs

130g plain flour

90ml sunflower oil

8 sausages

Salt and pepper

For the onion gravy

1 tsp sunflower oil

1 medium onion, peeled and chopped into thin slices

1 tsp plain flour

1 tsp sugar

300ml hot vegetable stock

1 tsp Worcestershire sauce

Salt and pepper

Tip: Make sure the oil is really hot when pouring the batter into the tin. This will help it to rise.

* Preheat the oven to 200°C Fan/Gas Mark 7.

* Place the milk into a jug, crack in the eggs and whisk well.

* Sift the flour through a sieve into a bowl and season with salt and pepper. Pour in the milk and egg mixture.

* Whisk well until the batter is smooth and the flour is incorporated. Leave the batter to rest for 30 minutes before using.

* Pour the oil into a large non-stick roasting tin and place in the oven for 3–4 minutes to heat up.

* Add the sausages and bake for 15 minutes until they just start to brown, then remove the tin from the oven. Quickly, so the oil stays really hot, pour the batter into the tin around the sausages and put them back in the oven. Bake for 25–30 minutes until golden, well risen and crisp.

* Meanwhile, make the onion gravy. Heat the oil in a frying pan, add the onion and cook for 5 minutes until it starts to soften.

* Add the flour and sugar and stir to coat the onion. Pour in the stock and Worcestershire sauce and season with salt and pepper. Leave to bubble away gently until the toad in the hole is ready to serve.

* Serve the toad in the hole immediately with the onion gravy on the side.

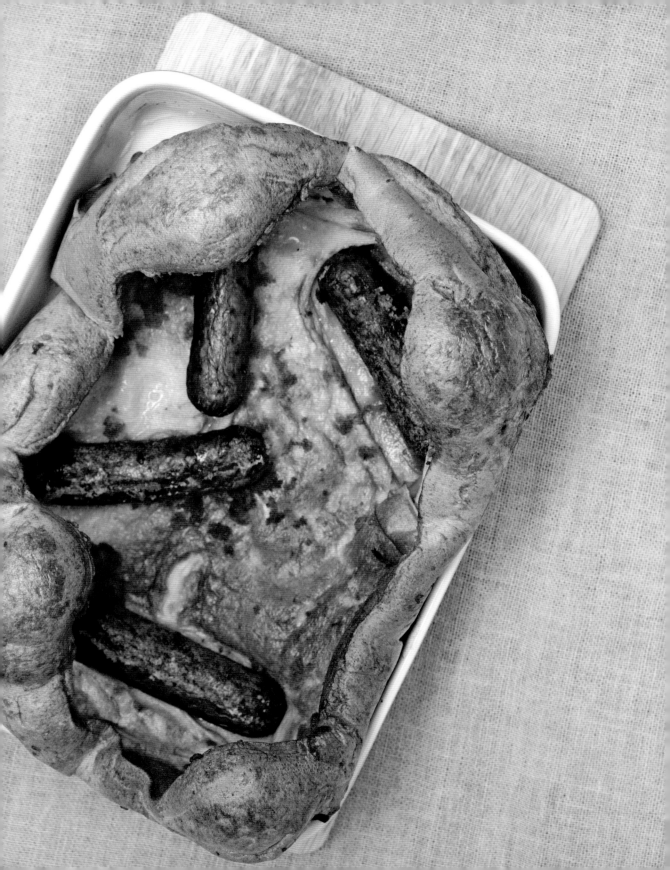

LAMB KEBABS

Serves: 4

These gorgeous kebabs are so simple to make and taste amazing served with roasted vegetables and flatbreads or pittas. Tzatziki also goes well with them (see page 114). In the summer, you can easily cook these on a barbecue instead of using the grill.

500g diced lamb leg

**2 garlic cloves,
peeled and crushed**

5 tbsp olive oil

Juice of ½ lemon

Salt and pepper

* Place the lamb chunks into a mixing bowl. Add the garlic, olive oil and lemon juice and season with salt and pepper.

* Cover with cling film and refrigerate for at least an hour.

* When you are ready to cook the kebabs, preheat the grill to a high temperature.

* Thread the lamb chunks evenly onto four skewers.

* Grill for 12–15 minutes, turning halfway through the time. Lamb is okay to eat even if it's slightly pink inside after this cooking time.

Tip: If you are using wooden skewers, soak them in water for at least 30 minutes beforehand so they don't burn while cooking.

LEMON AND HERB ROAST CHICKEN

Serves: 4–6

Roasting a chicken is a skill for life! This recipe makes it easy, and has lovely subtle flavours from the lemon and herbs. Great served with Rosemary and Garlic Roast Potatoes (page 154) and Honey Roast Parsnips (page 159).

1.5–1.7kg roasting chicken

1 lemon

Sprigs fresh thyme or parsley (or 1 tbsp dried herbs)

75g salted butter

Tip: If you have any leftovers, the meat will work very well wherever chicken is required in any of the pasta, noodle, risotto, soup, salad, curry or panini dishes in this book.

* Preheat the oven to 190°C Fan/Gas Mark 6.

* Note the weight of the chicken. If you bought it from a supermarket, it may say the weight on the packaging. If you bought it from a butcher, get them to weigh it for you and write the weight on the bag. This will determine the cooking time. The chicken will take 20 minutes per 450g, plus an extra 20 minutes at the end. This means that a 1.5kg chicken will take 90 minutes.

* Cut the lemon in half and insert both halves into the chicken's cavity, along with the thyme or parsley. Rub the butter all over the top of the chicken, not forgetting the legs and wings. This will make the skin lovely and golden and crispy.

* Place the chicken in a large ovenproof baking dish or roasting tin with deep sides, and cover with foil. Bake in the oven for the time based on its weight, excluding the extra 20 minutes.

* After this time, remove the chicken from the oven, take off the foil and place it back in the oven for the remaining 20 minutes.

* When cooked, the skin should be golden and crispy and there should be lots of juices. To check that the meat is cooked through properly, stick a sharp knife into a leg and look at the colour of the juices running out. If they are clear, the chicken is cooked. If they are not, return the chicken to the oven for another 10 minutes and test again. No meat on the chicken should be pink, so do be observant when you are carving. If in doubt, cover it in foil and return to the oven again.

* Once the chicken is thoroughly cooked, cover it in foil, and then a clean tea towel to keep the heat in, and set aside for 10–15 minutes to relax before serving. This lets the meat become more tender, so be sure not to miss out this step.

ONE-TRAY ROAST PORK WITH APPLES AND ONIONS

Serves: 4

This delicious roast pork is great for feeding friends! The apples and onions add loads of flavour to the meat. A loin joint works particularly well, and pork is one of the cheaper roasting joints.

1kg joint of pork, skin on and scored (see Tip)

1 tbsp salt

4 eating apples, preferably a smaller variety such as Cox

2 large onions, peeled and cut into quarters, or 4 shallots, peeled and halved lengthways

Mashed potato, to serve

Tip: If you like crackling, buy a joint with well-scored skin (a butcher or supermarket meat-counter will do this for you if you ask).

* Preheat the oven to 230°C Fan/Gas mark 9.

* Place the joint of pork in a large roasting tray, skin-side up. Rub the salt all over the skin. Cook the meat in the oven for 25 minutes.

* After this time, turn the oven down to 190°C Fan/Gas Mark 6 and cook for a further 30 minutes per 450g. So a 1kg piece of meat would need to be cooked for a further 1 hour 5 minutes.

* When the meat has just 20 minutes remaining in the oven, place the apples and the onions or shallots in the tray with the pork and bake until the time on the meat is up.

* After this time test the pork by sticking a skewer or knife into the centre of the meat and looking at the juices running out – they should be clear. If not, return to the oven for another 5 minutes and test again.

* Once the meat is cooked, place it on a large plate and cover with foil, to allow it to rest and become more tender.

* Pour the juices from the roasting tray out into a jug, but retain the apples and onions in the tray and return them to the oven for a further 15 minutes. When they are done, remove from the tray, put them on a plate and cover with foil to keep warm.

* To make the gravy from the juices, first spoon off the fatty layer. If your roasting tin can go on the hob (metal or ceramic), pour the juices back into it. Otherwise, pour the juice into a saucepan. Heat the juices on the hob until they are bubbling, whisking continuously.

* To carve the pork, remove the crackling first and slice the meat, serving chunks of crackling on the side along with the roasted apples and onions, and the gravy. Serve with mash.

SALMON, SPINACH AND LEEK FILO PIE

Serves: 4–6

This yummy salmon pie is topped with filo pastry, which is much lighter and healthier than other types of pastry. To make this go far enough for six people, serve with plenty of veg and new potatoes.

For the cheese sauce

30g butter

30g plain flour

200ml milk

100g Cheddar cheese, grated

For the bake

45g butter

2 leeks, washed and sliced into 1cm thick rings

300g salmon fillets

150g frozen spinach (approximately 10 balls)

125g filo pastry (about 4 sheets)

Tip: If you don't have a pastry brush to spread the melted butter on the top of the pie, just dab it on with your fingers.

* Preheat the oven to 180°C Fan/Gas mark 6.

* Start with the cheese sauce. In a large saucepan, melt the butter on a gentle heat. Make sure you have a wooden spoon, a whisk and the milk measured out in a jug next to you.

* When all of the butter is melted, tip in the flour and stir it in quickly using the wooden spoon. It will look like a thick paste. Continue to stir vigorously for the next couple of minutes until the flour and butter paste starts to bubble.

* Then, pour in the milk, a little bit at a time, whisking vigorously after each addition until smooth. Keep whisking continuously.

* When all the milk has been added, the sauce should look smooth and glossy. Tip in the grated cheese and continue to whisk. Season with pepper only and let it bubble away gently for 4–5 minutes, whisking continuously.

* In a frying pan, melt the butter for the bake over a low heat. Pour around two-thirds into a bowl and set aside. Add the leek rings to the pan and cook for around 15 minutes on a low heat until the leek is nicely softened but not browned.

* Meanwhile, ensure the salmon is free from skin and bones and break the fillets into flakes, roughly 2.5cm.

* Arrange the flakes of salmon evenly in a large ovenproof baking dish. Next, add the balls of frozen spinach evenly and then the leek. Pour over the cheese sauce evenly.

* Take the first sheet of filo pastry and scrunch it lightly, then lay it over a quarter of the top of the pie. Repeat with the other sheets. Once the pie is completely covered, brush it with the reserved melted butter.

* Place the pie in the oven and bake for around 30 minutes until the top is a lovely deep golden brown and the cheese sauce is bubbling.

TOMATO AND ONION TART

Serves: 4 (Vegetarian)

This gorgeous-looking tart uses only simple ingredients, including ready-made pastry. It's quick to make and is bound to impress friends or parents. Serve with a big fresh salad.

375g packet of ready-rolled puff pastry

1 tbsp sun-dried tomato pesto or tomato purée

Splash of milk

15 cherry tomatoes, halved

½ large onion, peeled and sliced into 5mm thick rings

2 tbsp black olives, halved (optional)

50g Parmesan (or vegetarian equivalent), finely grated

* Preheat the oven to 180°C/Gas Mark 6.

* Unroll the puff pastry and place on a large baking sheet. If it does not fit, just halve it and make two tarts on two separate sheets.

* Use a sharp knife to score a border around the edge of the pastry rectangle, running roughly 2–3cm away from but parallel to the edge of the pastry.

* Spread the pesto or tomato purée inside the middle rectangle you have just marked out.

* Brush the milk around the outer border of pastry. If you don't have a pastry brush, just dab on the milk using a finger.

* Scatter the cherry tomatoes and onion rings over the pastry, along with the olives if you are using them.

* Sprinkle the Parmesan evenly over the top and bake for 18–20 minutes until the topping is nicely brown, and the edges of the pastry are browned and risen.

* Serve the tart immediately while hot, with salad and crusty bread if you are hungry.

SALADS, VEGGIES AND SIDES

GOAT'S CHEESE, PEAR AND WALNUT SALAD

Serves: 1 (Vegetarian)

This salad may look fancy but in fact only calls for a few simple ingredients, sliced up and tossed together. The pears and honey give it a nice sweet edge.

50g washed salad leaves

25g walnuts

25g goat's cheese,
cut into small pieces

½ ripe pear, cored and cut
into thin slices lengthways

2 tbsp olive oil

2 tsp lemon juice

1 tsp runny honey

Salt and pepper

* Place the salad leaves in a bowl. Scatter over the walnuts, pieces of goat's cheese and slices of pear.

* Whisk together the oil, lemon juice and honey in a small jug or cup. Season with salt and pepper.

* Pour the dressing over the salad and toss well.

* Serve immediately.

WALDORF SALAD

Serves: 1 (Vegetarian)

A fresh, crunchy salad of apple, celery and walnuts, which is so-called because it was first served at the Waldorf Hotel in New York, over 100 years ago.

2 celery sticks, thinly sliced

Handful of grapes, halved

½ eating apple, cored and cut
into 1cm cubes (skin on or
peeled – up to you)

Small handful of
walnut pieces

Small handful of sultanas

2 tsp mayonnaise

* Place all the ingredients into a bowl and mix well.

* Serve immediately on its own, with some lettuce or with bread on the side.

LENTIL, ROASTED VEGETABLE AND GOAT'S CHEESE SALAD

Serves: 1 (Vegetarian)

This vegetarian salad is healthy and full of flavour. For how to roast Mediterranean vegetables, see page 151 (this salad is a great way to use up leftovers from that recipe), or supermarkets sell bags of frozen chargrilled veg that can be used here instead.

A handful of lettuce leaves

75g pre-cooked puy lentils, from a pouch, or drained and rinsed if from a can (see Tip)

40g soft goat's cheese

½ quantity of cold Roasted Mediterranean Vegetables (page 151) or frozen chargrilled veg, defrosted

2 tsp olive oil

¼ tsp lemon juice

Salt and pepper

* Lay the lettuce leaves out onto a plate. Sprinkle over the lentils and crumble over the goat's cheese. If it's very soft, then just break off chunks.

* Scatter the roasted vegetables over the top of the salad.

* Make the dressing by whisking together the olive oil, lemon juice and salt and pepper in a small jug or cup.

* Drizzle the dressing over the salad just before serving.

Tip: It is much easier to buy puy lentils pre-cooked in pouches or cans than it is to cook your own from dried.

ROASTED VEGETABLE COUSCOUS

Serves: 2 (Vegetarian)

This filling couscous salad is perfect for a packed lunch, or as a side at a barbecue. It will keep for a few days in the fridge as long as you don't add the dressing. Instead of roasting fresh vegetables, you can use frozen chargrilled veg, available from supermarkets.

For the couscous

150g couscous

300ml hot vegetable stock

1 quantity of Roasted Mediterranean Vegetables (page 151) or frozen chargrilled veg, defrosted

For a dressing (optional)

50ml olive oil

Juice of ½ lime

Salt and pepper

* Place the couscous in a large bowl, pour in the hot stock and cover the bowl with cling film. Set aside for 5 minutes.

* If you are making the dressing, do so now. Place the oil, lime juice and salt and pepper in a small bowl and whisk well. Set aside.

* After 5 minutes, remove the cling film from the couscous and use a fork to fluff up the grains. All the water should be absorbed by now. If not, stir, cover again and leave for a further 5 minutes.

* Add the cooked roasted vegetables and stir in.

* Immediately before serving, pour over the dressing and stir well.

TUNA AND BEAN SALAD

Serves: 1

This store-cupboard salad can be thrown together if you keep cans of beans and tuna in the cupboard, and some green beans in the freezer.

½–1 can tuna, drained (depending on appetite)

200g canned mixed beans, drained and rinsed

A handful of cooked green beans

¼ red onion, peeled and finely chopped

2 tsp olive oil

1 tsp white wine vinegar

Salt and pepper

* Place the tuna, mixed beans, green beans and red onion into a bowl.

* In a small jug or cup, combine the olive oil and white wine vinegar, and season with salt and pepper. Whisk together well.

* Pour the dressing over the tuna and beans and stir well to combine.

* Serve immediately on its own or with salad leaves.

SUPERFOOD SALAD

Serves: 1 (Vegetarian)

Superfoods are ingredients which are considered highly nutritious and good for you. So this recipe is the perfect detox after a heavy weekend, and will definitely help you kick the Freshers' flu. It tastes so delicious – almost too good for something so healthy!

4 broccoli florets, halved

3 tbsp fresh or frozen peas

2 tbsp mixed seeds e.g. sunflower, sesame and pumpkin

75g feta cheese, crumbled

½ ripe avocado

1 tsp lemon juice

1 tbsp olive oil

Salt and pepper

* Half-fill a small saucepan with water and bring to the boil.

* When the water is boiling, add the broccoli florets and set a timer for 1 minute.

* After 1 minute, add the peas and cook with the broccoli for a further 3 minutes. (This will produce vegetables that still have some crunch. If you prefer your veg softer, cook for a further 2 minutes before draining.)

* Drain the vegetables immediately and run them under cold water in a colander. Set aside to cool.

* Add the seeds to a small dry frying pan. Toast on a medium heat for a minute or two. You should start to smell the seeds. Take care not to let them burn. Set aside once toasted.

* Place the crumbled feta in a bowl. Cut the avocado into 2cm chunks and add to the bowl.

* Add the drained vegetables and seeds to the bowl and mix well. Add the lemon juice and olive oil to the salad, sprinkle with salt and pepper, and serve immediately.

CAESAR SALAD

Serves: 1

This famous salad is often on restaurant menus but is super-easy to make at home. This recipe is big enough for a meal for one, or can be divided between a few people as a side. It can be made with or without the chicken. When looking for Cos lettuce at the shops, bear in mind it is sometimes called Romaine lettuce.

For the salad

½ Cos lettuce

50g cold chicken,
torn into pieces (optional)

50g croutons, either shop
bought or homemade
(see separate method)

25g Parmesan, finely grated

For the dressing

2 tbsp mayonnaise

1 tsp lemon juice

Salt

1 tsp olive oil

¼ garlic clove, peeled and
crushed, or use part of a
roasted clove of garlic

1 anchovy fillet,
finely chopped (optional)

* Lay out the lettuce on a plate. Top with the chicken, if using, and the croutons.

* Sprinkle over the Parmesan cheese.

* Make up the dressing by whisking all the ingredients together in a small jug or cup.

* Drizzle the dressing over the salad and dive in without delay.

Homemade croutons

Take a thick slice of ciabatta, sourdough or baguette. Place 2 tablespoons of olive oil in a pan and heat over a medium–high heat. Meanwhile, cut the bread up into 2cm chunks. Fry the croutons for around 3 minutes until golden and crunchy. Drain on kitchen paper and season with salt and pepper before using in the salad.

Tip: This is a great way to use up leftover roast chicken (see page 133). Cos lettuce is the traditional lettuce to use here, but any crisp lettuce will work instead.

CHICKEN CLUB SALAD

Serves: 1

Chicken, bacon and avocado were just made to go together, and this filling salad contains them all, along with a few other tasty fresh ingredients. Once made, serve immediately, as the avocado will go brown in a matter of minutes.

3½ tsp olive oil

2 rashers of bacon, cut into 1cm strips

75g cooked chicken, torn into pieces

1 tomato, chopped into 1cm chunks

1 small ripe avocado, chopped into 2cm chunks

50g lettuce leaves (about ½ small lettuce or 4–5 leaves from a large lettuce)

¼ tsp lemon juice

A handful of croutons (optional)

Salt and pepper

* Warm ½ teaspoon of the oil in a small saucepan over a medium heat. Add the bacon strips and cook for 10 minutes or so until the bacon is browned. Leave to cool for about 10 minutes.

* While the bacon is cooking, mix the chicken, tomato, avocado and lettuce leaves together in a bowl.

* Whisk the remaining olive oil, the lemon juice, salt and pepper together in a small jug or cup.

* Place the bacon on top of the salad. Drizzle over the dressing, sprinkle some croutons on top if you wish, and enjoy straight away.

Tip: A sprinkling of croutons makes this salad extra-special. See page 148 for how to make your own.

POTATO SALAD

Serves: 2 (Vegetarian)

A simple combination of new potatoes and mayonnaise, this is great for packed lunches, barbecues or as a quick side. It keeps extremely well for up to 3 days in the fridge.

300g waxy potatoes (such as Charlotte variety), halved
1 tbsp mayonnaise
1 spring onion, chopped finely
Salt and pepper

Tip: Little waxy new potatoes or salad potatoes are best to use here.

* Place the potatoes in a large saucepan filled with cold water.

* Bring to the boil on a fairly high heat (making sure it does not boil over), and cook for around 15 minutes until the potatoes are tender. You can check this by sticking a sharp knife into them. If it goes in easily, they are cooked, if you meet a little resistance, leave the potatoes to boil for another 2 minutes and test again. Be careful not to overcook the potatoes, or they may disintegrate. Once cooked, drain and leave to cool.

* Place the mayonnaise and spring onion in a large mixing bowl, add the cooled potatoes and stir well to coat each piece of potato in mayonnaise.

* Season with salt and pepper and serve.

COLESLAW

Serves: 4 as a side (Vegetarian)

Once you've tried making coleslaw for yourself you'll never buy shop-bought again! It is so much nicer, and really cheap too.

2 medium carrots, peeled
½ white cabbage
1 tsp salt
½ tsp sugar
1 tsp white wine vinegar
2½ tbsp mayonnaise

* Grate the carrots as finely as you can and set aside in a bowl.

* Using a sharp knife, cut the cabbage into very fine strips. (You can use a grater to do this if it is easier, and most food processors have a grating function too, if you have one.)

* Add the carrots and cabbage to the bowl.

* Next, add the salt, sugar and the vinegar and stir well to mix it through evenly.

* Finally, stir through the mayonnaise and tuck in straight away!

ROASTED MEDITERRANEAN VEGETABLES

Serves: 2 (Vegetarian)

Roasted vegetables are lovely as a simple side, but also great added to pasta, thrown into a salad, or even in sandwiches. The combination of vegetables used here is one of the cheapest, but you can experiment with whatever you fancy. Aubergines also work well. It's a great way to use up any veg that is going soft.

1 red onion, peeled and chopped into quarters

1 red, orange or yellow pepper, deseeded and chopped into 2cm chunks

2 large tomatoes, cut into quarters

1 courgette, cut into 1cm thick slices

1 tbsp olive oil

1 tsp dried mixed herbs or fresh rosemary or thyme

Salt and pepper

* Preheat the oven to 200°C Fan/Gas Mark 7.

* Place the prepared vegetables in a large mixing bowl. Pour over the olive oil, add the herbs and season with salt and pepper. Stir well to coat the vegetables thoroughly.

* Tip the vegetables out onto a large roasting tray and bake for 25–35 minutes until the vegetables are soft and slightly crisp around the edges.

* Enjoy hot or cold. They will keep for 3 days in the fridge.

Tip: If you like garlic, you can place a couple of cloves still in their skins in the tray. Once roasted, peel away the skin and you will have some lovely soft roasted garlic to enjoy with your vegetables.

NIÇOISE SALAD

Serves: 1

This is a great option for when you don't have much fresh food in the fridge, as long as you keep your cupboard and freezer stocked up with basics. Fresh olives can be expensive, but you can just use olives from a can or jar, which are much more affordable.

3 small waxy potatoes, such as Charlotte variety

1 large egg

50g green beans, fresh or frozen

75g canned tuna, drained

5 pitted black olives

2 tbsp olive oil

1 tsp red wine vinegar

Salt and pepper

Tip: This salad keeps for a day in the fridge without the dressing, so you can prepare it in advance, but only add the dressing just before you eat.

* You can cook the potatoes, egg and beans at the same time in one pan as follows. Place the potatoes in a large saucepan of cold water and bring to the boil. Once boiling, set the timer for 8 minutes. After this time, add the egg and set the timer for 3 minutes. Then, add the beans and set the timer for 4 minutes. Finally, drain the lot well and let everything cool before using.

* Cut the boiled potatoes into quarters and place in a large bowl.

* Peel the egg, cut into quarters lengthways and add to the bowl with the drained tuna, cooked green beans and olives.

* In a small jug or cup, whisk the oil, vinegar and salt and pepper together and drizzle over the salad. Stir gently to combine all the ingredients evenly.

* Serve immediately.

ROSEMARY AND GARLIC ROAST POTATOES

Serves: 4 (Vegetarian)

These little roast potatoes are really delicious and a great way to jazz up a traditional roast dinner. If you can't get hold of fresh rosemary, dried is fine.

4 tbsp olive oil

900g potatoes, peeled and cut into 2.5cm pieces

6 garlic cloves, skin on

Leaves from 1 large rosemary sprig, or 1 tbsp dried rosemary

* Preheat the oven to 200°C Fan/Gas Mark 7.

* Add the olive oil to a large roasting tray. Place the tray in the oven for 3 minutes for the oil to heat up.

* Remove the tray from the oven with oven gloves, and place the potatoes into the hot oil. Turn them over using a spoon to ensure they are evenly coated in oil.

* Add the cloves of garlic to the tray, and sprinkle the rosemary leaves evenly over the potatoes.

* Bake for 45–60 minutes until the potatoes are really brown and crunchy.

* Serve immediately, with the roasted garlic cloves, which will be lovely and sweet.

Roast potatoes with bacon and onions

Follow the recipe above, but omit the garlic and lay 1 large onion, peeled and cut into eighths lengthways, in the tray instead. Bake for 25 minutes, then remove from the oven, turn the potatoes over to ensure they cook evenly, and lay 4 rashers of smoked back bacon on top of the potatoes. Bake for a further 20–35 minutes until the potatoes and onion are golden and the bacon is crisp.

PERFECT POTATO WEDGES

Serves: 1 (Vegetarian)

Wedges make a great side – they go with so many meals and are quite a bit healthier than chips. Multiply the quantities according to how many people you want to cook for.

1 large potato per person, weighing 150–300g
Sunflower oil
Salt and pepper

* Preheat the oven to 200°C Fan/Gas Mark 7.

* Bring a large saucepan of salted water to the boil.

* Cut the potato into chunky wedges (no need to peel it). You can do this by slicing the potato in half lengthways and then laying each half out on a board, cut-side down. Now cut each half into thirds, again lengthways, by cutting on an angle with your knife pointing towards the centre of the potato.

* Place the wedges into the boiling water and cook for 10 minutes until they start to soften, but are not completely cooked through.

* After this time, drain the wedges and set aside in a colander.

* Take a large roasting tray and add a couple of tablespoons of oil. Place the tray in the oven for around 3 minutes to heat up.

* Remove the tray from the oven and add the par-boiled potato wedges. Turn them over a few times to ensure they are well coated in oil. Season and return to the oven. Bake for around 30 minutes until they are well browned and crispy outside.

* Serve immediately.

MASHED POTATO

Serves: 2 (Vegetarian)

Here are two excellent ways to make mashed potato. Using milk and butter is more traditional, but olive oil works extremely well and is great if you don't eat dairy or if the fridge is really bare!

Dairy version

450g floury potatoes (such as Maris Piper, King Edward or Desiree), peeled and cut into 2cm chunks

50g butter

1 tbsp milk

Salt and pepper

Olive oil version

450g floury potatoes, peeled and cut into 2cm chunks

2 tsp olive oil

Salt and pepper

* Place the peeled potatoes in a large saucepan filled with cold water. Bring to the boil and cook for 12–16 minutes until the potatoes are tender. Test they are cooked by sticking a sharp knife into the potatoes. If it goes in easily, they are cooked. If you meet a little resistance, leave the potatoes to boil for another 2 minutes and test again. Once the potatoes are cooked, drain well and leave in the colander.

* Ensure all the water is drained from the saucepan you used to boil the potatoes. If going for the dairy version, place the milk and butter into the pan over a medium heat so that the butter is melted and the milk is warmed through. Add the drained potatoes and get stuck in with the potato masher.

* If you are making olive oil mash, put the potatoes back into the saucepan, ensuring you have poured out all the cooking water. Pour the olive oil over the potatoes and start to mash. You don't need to turn on the hob again while mashing with oil.

* Give the potatoes a good mash for a minute or so until they are really smooth. Season with salt and pepper and taste them to check they have enough salt and pepper (and butter, if using).

* Serve immediately.

Colcannon

To make colcannon, first make a quantity of mashed potato. Melt 1 teaspoon of butter in a frying pan over a medium heat. Add 100g of thinly sliced cabbage and 3 finely sliced spring onions and cook gently for 10 minutes or so until they are both softened. Place the cabbage and spring onion into a large bowl, followed by the hot mashed potato and stir together well. Serve immediately.

CAULIFLOWER CHEESE

Serves: 2–3 (Vegetarian)

Warm and comforting, cauliflower cheese is a cheap and delicious dish that's great as a side, or even better as a meal served with crusty bread and salad.

1 large cauliflower

25g butter

25g plain flour

500ml milk

150g mature Cheddar cheese, grated

Pinch of freshly grated nutmeg (optional, but nice)

50g Parmesan cheese (or vegetarian equivalent), grated

Salt and pepper

* Preheat the oven to 200°C Fan/Gas Mark 7.

* Fill a large saucepan with water, add a pinch of salt and bring up to the boil.

* Take the leaves off the cauliflower and cut the rest into florets and add to the water when boiling. Cook the cauliflower florets for 5 minutes until you can insert a sharp knife into the stalks without too much difficulty. Drain immediately.

* Make the cheese sauce by melting the butter in a medium saucepan over a low heat. Tip in the flour and stir for about 1 minute with a wooden spoon. It will look like a thick paste. Continue to stir vigorously for the next couple of minutes until the flour and butter paste starts to bubble.

* Then, pour in the milk, a little bit at a time, whisking vigorously after each addition until smooth. Keep whisking continuously.

* When all the milk has been added, the sauce should look smooth and glossy. Add the cheese and whisk gently until the cheese has melted in and the sauce is smooth. Season with pepper, a little salt and the nutmeg, if you are using it. Have a little taste – the sauce should have plenty of flavour. Add more seasoning if it needs it.

* Lay the cauliflower florets out into a medium-large ovenproof baking dish and pour the sauce over the top.

* Top with the Parmesan and bake for around 30 minutes until golden and bubbling.

YORKSHIRE PUDDINGS

Serves: 4 (Vegetarian)

Use a muffin tin to make individual puddings, or a large roasting tray to make one large Yorkshire pud to cut into portions. Getting the oil nice and hot before you add the batter is the key to success.

300ml full-fat milk

2 large eggs

130g plain flour

Salt and pepper

3 tbsp sunflower oil

* Pour the milk into a jug, crack in the eggs and whisk well. Sift the flour through a sieve into a bowl, season with salt and pepper and pour in the egg and milk mixture.

* Whisk well until the batter is smooth and the flour is incorporated. Leave the batter to rest for 30 minutes before using.

* Preheat the oven to 200°C Fan/Gas Mark 7. Place the oil in your chosen tin (see Introduction) and place in the oven for 3–4 minutes to heat up. Make sure the oil is really hot.

* Pour the batter into the tin and bake for 25–30 minutes for a large pudding, or 15–18 minutes for individual puddings, until golden, well risen and crisp. Serve immediately.

HOMEMADE APPLE AND HERB STUFFING

Serves: 4 (Vegetarian)

Stuffing is simple to make yourself and tastes much better than the instant mix. Use packet breadcrumbs or whiz up leftover or stale bread.

35g butter

½ small onion,
peeled and chopped

1 small eating apple,
chopped into 5mm cubes

60g breadcrumbs

1 tsp dried thyme or rosemary

Salt and pepper

* Melt the butter in a small frying pan over a medium heat. Add the onion and apple and fry until softened, but not coloured.

* Put the breadcrumbs and herbs into a mixing bowl. Season with salt and pepper and add the onion mixture, once softened. Stir all the ingredients together to form a moist mixture.

* If stuffing a chicken, push the mixture into the cavity, making sure not to pack it too tightly as it expands as it cooks. Add an extra 20–30 minutes onto the cooking time of your chicken.

* Otherwise, pinch off golfball-sized pieces and roll into smooth balls. Place in a buttered ovenproof dish and bake at 180°C Fan/Gas Mark 4 for 20–30 minutes until browned and firm.

HERBY ROAST CARROTS

Serves: 4 (Vegetarian)

A handful of thyme and a drizzle of olive oil really revs up plain carrots. These are delicious served with a roast dinner, pie or casserole.

12 large carrots, peeled and
cut into quarters lengthways

2 tsp dried thyme

3 tbsp olive oil

Salt and pepper

* Preheat the oven to 180°C Fan/Gas Mark 6.

* Lay the carrots out in a large roasting tray.

* Sprinkle over the thyme, drizzle over the olive oil and season with salt and pepper.

* Roast the carrots in the oven for 30–40 minutes until tender. Serve immediately.

HONEY ROAST PARSNIPS

Serves: 4 (Vegetarian)

This recipe takes parsnips to another level of deliciousness altogether!

60g butter

4 tbsp runny honey

8 parsnips, peeled and cut
into quarters lengthways

Salt and pepper

* Preheat the oven to 180°C Fan/Gas Mark 6.

* Melt the butter and honey together in a small saucepan on a low heat.

* Place the prepared parsnips in a large roasting tray and drizzle over the butter and honey mixture. Season with salt and pepper and toss well to ensure they are evenly coated.

* Bake for 20 minutes, remove from the oven, toss well again and bake for another 10–20 minutes until golden brown.

* Serve immediately.

GARLIC AND CHILLI BROCCOLI

Serves: 2–3 generously (Vegetarian)

Transform broccoli from boring to brilliant with these simple, flavoursome additions.

250g broccoli florets

2 garlic cloves, peeled and chopped finely

½ small fresh red chilli, chopped finely

25g butter

* Steam or boil the broccoli until it is nearly cooked, for around 4 minutes or so. You want it to be edible, but not too soft.

* Place the garlic and chilli in a frying pan with the butter. On a medium heat, cook until the butter has melted and you can smell the garlic cooking.

* Once the broccoli is sufficiently cooked, drain well and place in the frying pan with the garlic and chilli butter. Toss well.

* Serve immediately – this tastes much better when hot.

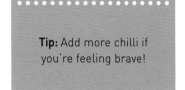

Tip: Add more chilli if you're feeling brave!

ROASTED GARLIC GREEN BEANS

Serves: 4 (Vegetarian)

Beans don't have to be boiled! Roasting them with garlic is a great way to perk them up. Use fresh beans or cook from frozen, it's up to you.

450g green beans, fresh or frozen

3 tbsp olive oil

3 garlic cloves, peeled and crushed

Salt and pepper

* Preheat the oven to 180°C Fan/Gas Mark 6.

* Cover a large baking sheet in foil. Lay the green beans out over the foil.

* Drizzle the olive oil over the beans, then sprinkle the garlic evenly over them, followed by the salt and pepper.

* Roast the beans in the oven for 8–10 minutes. Note that frozen beans will take closer to 10 minutes to cook.

* The beans are done when they are slightly firm and dry to touch. The garlic will be lightly browned and fragrant.

* Serve immediately.

EGG FRIED RICE

Makes: 2 large or 4 small portions (Vegetarian)

This takeaway classic is a great way to use leftover rice. Or cook extra rice with another meal so that you have some over for this dish.

500g cold cooked rice
(or 275g uncooked rice)

2 tbsp sunflower
or vegetable oil

2 large eggs, beaten

100g peas, cooked

1 tsp salt

2 spring onions, chopped

* If using uncooked rice, place in a large saucepan with boiling water and salt, bring to the boil, cover and cook for the time stated on the packet. Drain well once cooked and leave to cool.

* Heat the oil in a wok or a large frying pan over a medium heat. Add the cold rice to the pan. Toss it around for a few seconds and add the egg. Stir vigorously to ensure the egg is distributed through the rice.

* Add the peas and season with salt. Continue to stir until the egg is set. Serve in bowls with the spring onion scattered over the top.

PILAU RICE

Serves: 4 (Vegetarian)

An easy, tasty way to add some va va voom to plain rice.

240g basmati rice

20g butter

1 tsp cumin seeds

1 cinnamon stick

5 green cardamom pods

5 cloves

½ tsp ground turmeric

1 small onion, peeled
and chopped finely

400ml water

Pinch of salt

* Place the rice in a sieve and run cold water through it for a minute or so until it is well washed. Drain well.

* Melt the butter in a saucepan over a low heat. Add the spices and let them sizzle for few seconds until you can smell them.

* Add the chopped onion to the pan and cook for roughly 5 minutes on a low heat until it starts to turn golden.

* Add the rice to the pan and stir until the grains of rice are coated with butter.

* Add the water and the salt and bring to the boil. Place the lid on the pan and leave to cook on a medium heat for 14 minutes. Do not remove the lid during this cooking time.

* Check the rice is cooked by trying a grain. If it's not, leave it covered for another 3 minutes and test again.

* Serve with a curry of your choice.

IN BREAD AND ON TOAST

CROQUE MONSIEUR

Serves: 1

This is a posh name for a grilled cheese and ham sandwich! It's the ultimate snack and great for a quick lunch or speedy supper.

2 slices of bread

15g butter

½ tsp Dijon mustard

1 slice of good-quality ham

40g Gruyère or mature Cheddar cheese, finely grated

* Preheat the grill to a medium–high temperature.

* Lightly toast the two slices of bread on both sides under the grill or in a toaster.

* Spread the toast with butter and mustard and put under the grill for another 30 seconds.

* Place the ham on one slice of the bread, on the side that has been spread with butter and mustard, then put half the cheese on top of the ham.

* Place the second slice of toast on top, buttered-side down. Top with the remaining cheese and grill for 2–3 minutes until the cheese is golden and bubbling. Serve immediately.

CROQUE MADAME

Serves: 1

A croque madame is the same thing as the croque monsieur above but with a fried egg on top.

2 slices of bread

25g butter

1 egg

½ tsp Dijon mustard

1 slice of good-quality ham

40g Gruyère cheese or mature Cheddar, finely grated

* Preheat the grill to a medium–high temperature.

* Lightly toast the two slices of bread on both sides under the grill or in a toaster.

* Melt 10g of butter in a small frying pan. Crack in the egg and cook for 3–4 minutes on a medium heat until the white has crisped up around the edges.

* Spread the toast with butter and mustard and put under the grill for 30 seconds. Place the ham on one slice, on the side with butter and mustard, then put half the cheese on top of the ham. Put the second slice of toast on top, buttered-side down.

* Top with the remaining cheese and grill for 2–3 minutes until the cheese is golden and bubbling. Serve with the egg on top.

FALAFEL AND TZATZIKI WRAP

Serves: 1 (Vegetarian)

Tzatziki is a cucumber yoghurt dip that goes deliciously with falafel. See page 114 if you want to try making your own.

1 tortilla wrap
2–3 falafel, depending on size
Couple of salad leaves
4 thin slices of peeled cucumber
2 tsp tzatziki (shop bought or see page 114)

* Place the tortilla wrap onto a plate.

* Place the falafel, salad leaves and cucumber in the centre of the wrap, dollop the tzatziki on top and roll up, making sure you fold in both ends.

* Cut in half and either eat right away or wrap in foil for a packed lunch.

AÏOLI CHICKEN SALAD WRAP

Serves: 1

Aïoli is a fancy name for garlic mayonnaise. It goes beautifully with many things: salad, chips, steak, burgers, as a dip, and of course in this wrap.

1 tortilla wrap
1 heaped tsp aïoli (see separate method below)
50g cooked chicken, torn into pieces
Couple of salad leaves
½ spring onion, finely chopped
4 thin slices of peeled cucumber

* Place the tortilla wrap onto a plate. Spoon the aïoli onto the wrap and spread evenly.

* Place the cooked chicken, salad leaves, chopped spring onion and cucumber in the centre of the wrap and roll up, making sure you fold in both ends.

* Cut in half and either eat right away or wrap in foil for a packed lunch.

Homemade aïoli

This recipe serves 2. Place 2 peeled and finely chopped garlic cloves into a bowl with a pinch of salt and crush together. Add 1 egg yolk and whisk into the garlic well. Pour in 200ml of sunflower or olive oil, a little at a time, and whisk well after each addition. If you have an electric whisk or food processor, it is worth using it here. Continue to add the oil, little by little, and whisk vigorously until the aïoli thickens and all the oil has been incorporated. Keep refrigerated and eat within 2 days.

SWEET CHILLI PRAWN WRAP

Serves: 1

This zingy wrap is best eaten straight away and isn't ideal for a packed lunch because prawns need to be kept refrigerated.

1 tsp mayonnaise
½ tsp sweet chilli sauce
50g cooked prawns
1 tortilla wrap
Few lettuce leaves

* Place the mayonnaise and sweet chilli sauce into a small bowl and mix together well.

* Stir in the prawns.

* Place the tortilla wrap on to a plate and spoon the prawn mayonnaise mixture into the middle.

* Top with a few lettuce leaves and roll up, making sure you fold in both ends.

* Cut in half and eat straight away.

GARLIC MUSHROOM, AVOCADO AND MOZZARELLA WRAP

Serves: 1 (Vegetarian)

Lovely eaten warm, this wrap contains a delicious combination of soft, mild ingredients.

Knob of butter
3–4 mushrooms, thinly sliced
1 garlic clove,
peeled and finely chopped
1 tortilla wrap
½ avocado, thinly sliced
50g mozzarella (approximately
½ ball), torn into chunks

* Melt the butter in a saucepan over a medium heat. Add the mushrooms, garlic and butter and cook for 4–5 minutes until the garlic is cooked and the mushrooms have softened. Discard any water that may have come out of the mushrooms.

* Place the tortilla wrap onto a plate with the hot mushrooms in the centre.

* Top with sliced avocado and chunks of mozzarella.

* Roll up and fold in both ends. Enjoy while the mushrooms are warm.

FISH FINGER WRAP

Serves: 1

As a kid, you might have had fish fingers with potato waffles, but this is the 21st century way to eat them! You can use shop-bought fish fingers or make your own as directed below. Delicious served warm and drizzled with mayo or your favourite sauce.

2–3 fish fingers, shop-bought or homemade (see below)

1–2 tsp sunflower oil

1 tortilla wrap (shop-bought or see page 121)

Some salad (lettuce leaves, cucumber, tomato and/or red onion slices)

Mayonnaise, aïoli (shop-bought or see page 166), tomato ketchup or sweet chilli sauce

* If using shop-bought fish fingers, place into a frying pan with the oil and gently fry for 12–16 minutes, or according to the packet instructions, until the fish fingers are thoroughly cooked through.

* Take the tortilla wrap and set out on a plate. Place the cooked fish fingers in the centre, top with salad and a sauce of your choice. Roll up the wrap, making sure you fold in both ends.

* Cut in half and enjoy while it's hot.

Homemade fish fingers

Set out three plates on the kitchen counter. On the first, sprinkle 1 tablespoon of plain flour, on the second pour 1 beaten egg, and on the third, spread 2 tablespoons dried breadcrumbs. Pour 200ml of sunflower oil into a frying pan and start to warm on a medium heat. Cut 200g of skinned and boned white fish into strips. Take the fish, a piece at a time, and roll it in the flour, then the egg and finally the breadcrumbs. Place the breadcrumbed fish into the pan and repeat with the other strips. Cook the fish fingers on a medium to high heat for 3–4 minutes on each side until golden brown. Serve straight away.

MOZZARELLA, CHICKEN AND PESTO PANINI

Serves: 1

Save cash on buying lunch out by making your own panini at home.
Cold roast chicken or shop-bought pieces are a quick filling here.

1 panini roll
1–2 tsp basil pesto
50g mozzarella, sliced
25g cooked chicken,
torn into pieces

* Preheat the grill to high.

* Cut the panini roll in half. Toast the outside of the halves
lightly until warm. Turn both pieces over and toast the insides.
This will help keep the filling hot.

* Spread the pesto inside the roll. Fill with mozzarella and chicken.

* Close the roll, press down and grill for 3–4 minutes until the
cheese is melted and bubbling.

* Cut in half and eat straight away.

BLT PANINI

Serves: 1

The world's favourite sandwich is even better served hot and grilled!

2 rashers of back bacon
1 panini roll
1 tsp mayonnaise
1 large lettuce leaf
½ medium ripe tomato, sliced

* Preheat the grill to high.

* Place the bacon rashers on a sheet of foil on a baking tray or
grillpan. Grill the bacon for around 2–3 minutes on each side
until the fat is crispy.

* Cut the panini roll in half. Toast the outside of the halves
lightly until warm. Turn both pieces over and toast the insides.
This will help keep the filling hot.

* Spread the mayonnaise inside the roll and fill with lettuce,
tomato and the cooked bacon.

* Close the roll, press down and grill for 3–4 minutes until the
filling is warmed through.

* Cut in half and eat straight away.

CORONATION CHICKEN PANINI

Serves: 1

This cheat's version of coronation chicken is fruity, delicious and great eaten warm.

50g cooked chicken, torn into pieces

1 tbsp mayonnaise

2 heaped tsp mango chutney

15g sultanas

1 panini roll

* Preheat the grill to high. Place the chicken, mayonnaise, mango chutney and sultanas in a bowl and mix to combine.

* Cut the panini roll in half. Toast the outside of the halves lightly until warm. Turn both pieces over and toast the insides. This will help keep the filling hot.

* Spread the chicken mixture inside the roll, then close the roll, press down and grill for 3–4 minutes until the filling is warmed through.

* Cut in half and eat straight away.

GOAT'S CHEESE, OLIVE AND SPINACH PANINI

Serves: 1 (Vegetarian)

If you enjoy strong flavours, this is the panini for you.

1 panini roll

50g soft goat's cheese

4 pitted black olives, sliced in half

Small handful of fresh baby spinach leaves

Salt and pepper

* Preheat the grill to high.

* Cut the panini roll in half. Toast the outside of the halves lightly until warm. Turn both pieces over and toast the insides. This will help keep the filling hot.

* Spread the goat's cheese inside the roll. Season with salt and pepper.

* Fill the roll with the olives and spinach leaves.

* Close the roll, press down and grill for 3–4 minutes until the filling is warmed through.

* Cut in half and eat straight away

PEA AND PARMESAN CROSTINI

Serves: 1 (Vegetarian)

Peas and Parmesan cheese are a match made in heaven. This is
a great snack to rustle up when the cupboard is practically bare.

50g frozen peas

2 slices of ciabatta
bread or baguette

1 tbsp finely grated
Parmesan cheese
(or vegetarian equivalent)

1 tsp olive oil

Salt and pepper

* Start by cooking the peas. Either boil in a saucepan with a
  little water for around 5 minutes or place them in a small
  bowl with 2 tablespoons of water and microwave until tender.
  Drain well.

* Put the bread on to toast, either under a hot grill or in a toaster.

* Meanwhile, place the peas in a bowl with the Parmesan and
  olive oil and season with salt and pepper. Mash together well.

* When the toast is golden, spread with the pea topping and
  enjoy while it is still hot.

TOMATO BRUSCHETTA

Serves: 1 (Vegetarian)

The classic Italian starter of juicy tomatoes on garlic toast! Great for a
simple lunch, supper or snack.

4 cherry tomatoes

2 tsp olive oil

2 slices of ciabatta bread
or baguette

1 small garlic clove, peeled

Few fresh basil leaves
(optional)

Salt and pepper

* Chop up the cherry tomatoes into small pieces. Place into a
  bowl, drizzle over a teaspoon of olive oil and season with salt
  and pepper. Mix well.

* Toast the slices of bread. Once they are golden brown,
  use the clove of garlic to rub over one side of each slice of bread.

* Drizzle the remaining olive oil over the same side of the
  pieces of toast.

* Now, spoon the tomatoes on top of the toast. Top with fresh
  basil leaves if you are using them and serve immediately.

CHEESE AND LEEK RAREBIT

Serves: 1–2 (Vegetarian)

An obvious late-night snack, rarebit is the ultimate cheese on toast. Leeks are a nice way to add some extra flavour.

½ tsp butter

¼ leek, washed and sliced thinly

2 large, thick slices of bread

1 medium egg

90g Chedddar cheese, grated

Salt and pepper

* Melt the butter in a small frying pan over a medium heat. Add the leek and cook for around 10 minutes until it's really nice and soft. Be careful not to let it brown too much.

* Meanwhile, preheat the grill, place the bread on the grill tray and toast on both sides. When done, set the tray aside somewhere safe like on top of the oven.

* Crack the egg into a bowl. Add the grated cheese, salt and pepper and whisk together well.

* When the leek is cooked, place it in the bowl with the egg and cheese and stir in.

* Top the toasted bread on the grill tray with this mixture.

* Transfer the toast back under the hot grill and toast for 2–3 minutes until the topping is bubbling and golden brown.

* Enjoy right away, while it's hot.

CHEESE AND BEER RAREBIT

Serves: 1–2 (Vegetarian)

Beer and cheese go brilliantly, especially melted together on toast!

2 large, thick slices of bread

1 medium egg

90g Chedddar cheese, grated

1 tbsp strong good-quality beer or stout

Salt and pepper

* Preheat the grill, place the bread on the grill tray and toast on both sides.

* Crack the egg into a bowl. Add the grated cheese, beer, salt and pepper and whisk together well.

* Top the toasted bread on the grill tray with this mixture.

* Transfer the toast back under the hot grill and toast for 2–3 minutes until the topping is bubbling and golden brown.

* Enjoy immediately.

POSH BEANS ON TOAST

Serves: 1 (Vegetarian)

This Italian-inspired version of beans on toast tastes great and will keep you going for ages.

1 tbsp olive oil

1 garlic clove, peeled and crushed

100g canned cannellini or borlotti beans, drained and rinsed

100g canned chopped tomatoes

2 slices of ciabatta bread or baguette

1 tbsp grated Parmesan cheese (or vegetarian equivalent)

Salt and pepper

* Warm the olive oil in a small saucepan over a gentle heat. Add the garlic and cook slowly until it becomes fragrant.

* Add the beans and tomatoes and stir. Season with salt and pepper and allow to cook for 5 minutes or so, until the beans are heated through.

* Toast the bread until golden, then top with the bean mixture.

* Sprinkle the Parmesan cheese on top and enjoy straight away.

MUSHROOMS ON TOAST

Serves: 1 (Vegetarian)

Buttery garlic mushrooms are really moreish and make a wonderful toast topper. Use large flat mushrooms for the best flavour.

15g butter

1 garlic clove, peeled and crushed

100g mushrooms, sliced thinly

½ tsp dried thyme

2 slices of ciabatta bread or baguette

Salt and pepper

* Melt the butter in a saucepan over a medium heat. Add the garlic and cook for a minute or two until fragrant.

* Add the mushrooms. Stir to ensure the mushrooms become well coated in melted butter.

* Season the mushrooms with thyme, salt and pepper and cook for around 15 minutes. Make sure any water from the mushrooms is cooked off.

* Toast the bread and top with the cooked mushrooms. Enjoy immediately!

THE MORNING
AFTER

CINNAMON FRENCH TOAST

Serves: 2 (Vegetarian)

This is an indulgent weekend breakfast of sweet fried bread, which is very easy to rustle up using just a few simple ingredients.

For the French toast

2 large eggs

1 tsp vanilla extract

60ml double cream

1½ tsp ground cinnamon

2 tsp icing sugar

2 slices of thick white bread or brioche

25g butter

For sprinkling

35g caster sugar

2 tsp ground cinnamon

* Beat the eggs in a bowl. Add the vanilla extract, cream, cinnamon and icing sugar and whisk together well. Pour this mixture into a large shallow bowl.

* Place the slices of bread into the creamy mixture and leave to sit for 3 minutes on each side so the bread soaks up the mixture.

* Once you have turned over the bread to soak on the second side, place the butter in a large frying pan and allow to melt over a gentle heat.

* Place the slices of bread into the pan, turn up the heat to a medium temperature and allow the toast to cook until golden on both sides.

* While the toast is cooking, mix the caster sugar and cinnamon together in a small cup. Sprinkle over each slice of French toast and serve immediately.

INSTANT PANCAKE MIX

Makes: 10 large pancakes (Vegetarian)

Keep this basic mix at the ready and you can rustle up some pancakes in just minutes, no matter how tired or hungover you may be. Prepare a batch of the mix by measuring out the ingredients and storing in a jam jar until needed. This recipe makes thin, crêpe-style pancakes.

For the instant pancake mix
200g plain flour

½ tsp salt

2 tsp caster sugar

To make up the pancakes
1 x batch of instant pancake mix

400ml milk

3 medium eggs

Knob of butter, for cooking

Tip: Instead of lemon juice and sugar, why not try clementine juice and caster sugar. Other suggestions are jam, Nutella, sliced banana and grated chocolate, peanut butter and banana, canned caramel, berries and whipped cream, honey, maple syrup or golden syrup, or cinnamon and caster sugar.

* To make the instant pancake mix, sift the flour, salt and caster sugar through a sieve into a bowl. Stir well and transfer to a jar or an airtight container until needed.

* To make up the pancakes, place the pancake mix into a large mixing bowl. Make a well in the centre.

* Pour the correct amount of milk into a measuring jug. Add the eggs and whisk together.

* Pour the milk and egg mixture into the pancake mix and whisk together until smooth. Pour the mixture back into the jug.

* Melt the butter in a non-stick frying pan over a medium to high heat, swirling it around until the pan is hot enough that the butter starts to bubble.

* Pour in just enough batter to thinly cover the base of the pan. Swirl round and leave the batter to cook for around 30–45 seconds. Lift up a corner of the pancake using a fish slice or palette knife. The underside should be lightly browned when ready to flip. Flip the pancake using the fish slice or, if you're brave enough, give it a quick flick.

* Cook the pancake for another 20–30 seconds on the other side until golden.

* Serve piping hot with your favourite toppings.

AMERICAN PANCAKES

Makes: six 7–10cm pancakes (Vegetarian)

Pancakes are such a treat in the morning. The good news is that they hardly require any cooking skills or time to make. Try them topped with berries and icing sugar or stir a few blueberries into the batter before cooking if you fancy something a little different.

135g plain flour

½ tsp salt

1 tbsp caster sugar

1 tsp baking powder

145ml milk

1 medium egg

Knob of butter, for cooking

Maple syrup, to serve

Berries or other toppings, as desired

Icing sugar, to dust (optional)

* In a bowl, combine the flour, salt, sugar and baking powder, and stir them together evenly.

* Measure out the milk into a measuring jug. Crack in the egg and whisk together using a fork. When well mixed, pour this mixture into the bowl containing the dry ingredients.

* Stir the mixture together gently until all the flour is mixed in. Don't worry about any lumps.

* Set the mixture aside for 10 minutes.

* Melt the butter in a large frying pan over a low heat and swirl it around so that the base of the pan is evenly covered in butter. Now, turn the heat up so that the pan starts to become quite hot.

* Pour in a couple of dollops of mixture at a time – roughly 2 heaped tablespoons. Leave the pancakes to cook without touching them for a minute or two until you notice several holes developing on the surface. Now you are ready to flip the pancakes.

* Cook for another couple of minutes on the other side until they are brown on both sides.

* Drizzle with maple syrup and serve with your topping of choice, such as fresh berries. Dust with icing sugar if desired.

FULL ENGLISH OMELETTE

Serves: 1 generously

If you enjoy a cooked breakfast in the morning, this is a great all-in-one version!

1 tsp olive oil

2 chipolata sausages

2 rashers of back bacon, cut into 1cm strips

4 cherry tomatoes

3 large eggs, beaten with a pinch of salt

* In a small saucepan, warm the oil over a medium heat. Add the sausages and cook for 3 minutes, and then add the bacon. Cook for a further 5 minutes until the sausages and bacon are browned.

* Add the tomatoes and pour in the eggs, then let the omelette cook for around 5 minutes on a medium heat. During this time, run a spatula around the edges to ensure the egg doesn't stick, and swirl the pan every minute or so to allow liquid egg to reach the edges and cook. Make sure the hob isn't too hot, or the base will burn. The omelette is ready to turn when there is only a small amount of liquid egg left on top.

* Turn the omelette over very carefully by placing a large plate over the pan. Make sure you wear oven gloves. Flip quickly onto the plate and slide it back, cooked-side up, into the pan.

* Cook for a further 2 minutes until it is cooked through. You can check this by cutting into the centre with a sharp knife to see if the middle is still runny. If it's not properly set, allow to cook for a further minute and check again. Serve immediately

POACHED EGG ON TOAST

Serves: 1 (Vegetarian)

A poached egg on toast with a warm, runny yolk makes a near-perfect breakfast. It's important to use the freshest eggs you can, as the whites hold together much better.

1 egg

Buttered toast, to serve

Fill a frying pan with water to a depth of 3cm. Bring to the boil, then crack in one large egg. Turn the heat down so that the egg gently simmers in the water for 4 minutes. Carefully scoop out the egg using a fish slice. Make sure you drain off any excess water then serve the poached egg on hot, buttered toast.

SCRAMBLED EGGS WITH BACON AND MUSHROOMS

Serves: 1

A couple of delicious additions make these the ultimate scrambled eggs.

20g butter

100g mushrooms

2 rashers of bacon
(ideally back bacon)

2 large eggs

2 tbsp milk

Salt and pepper

Buttered toast, to serve

Tip: There are different types of bacon to choose from: back bacon and streaky bacon, smoked and unsmoked. Streaky bacon has more fat running through it than back bacon, and generally crisps up better. Smoked bacon usually has more flavour than unsmoked. Cheaper bacon can contain extra water to bulk it up, whereas more premium bacon will not shrink when you cook it – worth buying if you can afford it.

* Melt 10g of the butter in a saucepan over a medium heat. Add the mushrooms and stir to ensure they become well coated in melted butter.

* Cook for around 15 minutes. Make sure any water from the mushrooms is cooked off.

* Meanwhile, preheat the grill to high. Place the bacon rashers on a sheet of foil on a grillpan or baking tray. Grill the bacon for around 2–3 minutes on each side until the fat is crispy.

* While the mushrooms and bacon are cooking, make the scrambled eggs. Crack the eggs into a bowl. Add the milk and season with salt and pepper. Whisk until well combined.

* Melt the remaining butter gently in a non-stick saucepan. Swirl around the pan.

* Pour the egg mixture into the pan over a medium heat. Stir continuously until the eggs are scrambled to your liking. For just-set, softly scrambled eggs, they'll take about 30 seconds, or for a firmer set, cook for 1 minute. Remove from the heat a moment or two before they're cooked to your liking as they will continue to cook in the residual heat of the pan.

* Serve the scrambled eggs on hot buttered toast with the bacon and mushrooms on the side.

FRUITY BIRCHER MUESLI

Serves: 1 (Vegetarian)

If you want a healthy and filling breakfast to set you up for the day, try Bircher muesli, a combination of soaked oats and fresh fruit. It's quicker to prepare than porridge and you also get one of your 5-a-day!

60g porridge oats

50ml fruit juice (apple or orange work nicely)

1 eating apple, grated

1 tbsp yoghurt

1 tsp honey or maple syrup

* The night before you want to eat this, place the oats and fruit juice together in a small bowl. Stir, cover with cling film, and leave in the fridge overnight.

* When you are ready for breakfast, grate an apple onto the juice-soaked oats. Spoon over the yoghurt and pour over the honey or syrup.

* Eat straight away as the apple will brown quickly if left.

Tip: To make this extra special, top with dried fruit and nuts too, such as almonds and dried apricots.

BREAKFAST BURRITOS

Serves: 1 (Vegetarian)

Roll up, roll up! These warm egg burritos are perfect if you like a bit of spice to wake your tastebuds in the morning. If you prefer your food a little milder just leave out the jalapeños and hot sauce.

2 large eggs

2 tbsp milk

10g butter

1 tortilla wrap
(shop-bought or see page 121)

¼ red pepper, finely chopped

1 small tomato, chopped

1 tsp chopped jalapeño peppers

1 tbsp grated mature
Cheddar cheese

Hot sauce, to serve (optional)

Salt and pepper

* Crack the eggs into a bowl. Add the milk and season with salt and pepper. Whisk until well combined.

* Melt the butter gently in a non-stick saucepan. Swirl around the pan.

* Pour the egg mixture into the pan over a medium heat. Stir continuously until the eggs are scrambled to your liking. For just-set, softly scrambled eggs, they'll take about 30 seconds, or for a firmer set, cook for 1 minute. Remove from the heat a moment or two before they're cooked to your liking as they will continue to cook in the residual heat of the pan.

* Place the tortilla onto a large plate. Transfer the eggs to the centre of the wrap. Add the chopped pepper, tomato and the jalapeños and sprinkle some cheese on top.

* Roll up the tortilla and tuck in the ends to form a burrito.

* Cut in half and eat without delay, with some hot sauce on the side if you like.

CHEDDAR AND BACON BREAKFAST MUFFINS

Makes: 12 muffins

If you like something savoury in the morning, try these gorgeous cheesy muffins. They're easy to make and the hardest thing will be stopping your housemates from gobbling them all up!

½ tsp sunflower oil

175g smoked back bacon (around 6 rashers), cut into 1cm pieces

285g plain flour

2 heaped tsp baking powder

½ tsp English mustard powder (optional)

75g cold unsalted butter, cut into cubes

250ml milk

1 large egg

225g mature Cheddar cheese, grated

Salt and pepper

* Preheat the oven to 180°C Fan/Gas Mark 6. Line a muffin tray with muffin cases. Set aside.

* Heat the oil in a small frying pan over a medium–hot heat. Add the bacon and cook until it is browned at the edges.

* Meanwhile, sift the flour, baking powder and mustard powder, if you're using it, through a sieve into a large mixing bowl. Season with salt and pepper and stir well.

* Add the butter and rub into the flour using your fingertips until the mixture looks like fine breadcrumbs.

* Pour the milk into a jug. Add the egg and whisk together well. Pour into the flour and butter mixture with 200g of the grated Cheddar and the cooked bacon. Gently fold all the ingredients together until just combined. Do not stir too much or the muffins will turn out heavy and dense.

* Divide the mixture evenly among the muffin cases. It is normal for the batter to be quite stiff at this stage.

* Sprinkle the remaining 25g of Cheddar evenly over the top of the muffins.

* Bake for 20–25 minutes until golden brown and well risen.

* Transfer the muffins to a wire rack to cool. They should be cool enough to eat after around 20 minutes.

CARROT, APPLE AND SULTANA MUFFINS

Makes: 12 muffins or 18 fairy cake-sized muffins (Vegetarian)

Packed full of good things, these unusual muffins are sweet and moist and make a great start to the day.

300g self-raising flour
1 tsp baking powder
1 tbsp ground cinnamon
Pinch of salt
275g caster sugar
4 large eggs
150ml sunflower oil
1 tbsp vanilla extract
200g carrots, peeled and grated
225g apple, peeled and grated
100g sultanas

* Preheat the oven to 170°C Fan/Gas Mark 5. Line your muffin or fairy cake tray with the appropriately sized cake cases.

* Sift the flour, baking powder, cinnamon and salt through a sieve into a large mixing bowl. Add the sugar and stir to combine.

* Place the eggs, oil and vanilla extract into a jug and whisk well.

* Stir the grated carrot, apple and sultanas into the jug. Pour this wet mixture into the dry mixture in the mixing bowl, and then stir gently to combine. Do not stir too much or the muffins will turn out heavy and dense.

* Divide the mixture evenly among the cake cases and bake for 20–25 minutes until risen and golden brown.

* Leave the muffins to cool in the tins for at least 20 minutes after removing from the oven. Then transfer them in their cases to a wire rack to cool fully.

SUMMER BERRY AND OAT MUFFINS

Makes: 12 muffins or 16 fairy cake-sized muffins (Vegetarian)

Lovely and fruity but not overly sweet, these muffins are packed with oats, which makes them substantial enough to stave off any mid-morning hunger pangs.

325g plain flour

1½ tbsp baking powder

Pinch of bicarbonate of soda

Pinch of salt

200g light brown soft sugar

50g porridge oats

2 medium eggs

100ml milk

100g natural yoghurt

75ml sunflower oil

1 tsp vanilla extract

125g summer berries (blueberries, raspberries and blackberries are lovely)

* Preheat the oven to 180°C Fan/Gas Mark 6. Line your muffin tray with the appropriately sized cake cases.

* Sift the flour, baking powder, bicarbonate of soda and salt through a sieve into a large mixing bowl. Add the sugar and oats and stir in.

* Put the eggs, milk, yoghurt, oil and vanilla extract into a jug and whisk together well.

* Pour the wet ingredients into the dry and gently stir to combine. Try not to mix too much or the muffins will turn out heavy and dense. Add the berries and gently stir in to the mixture.

* Divide the muffin mixture evenly among the cake cases and bake for 20–25 minutes for muffins and 15–20 minutes for fairy cakes until golden brown.

* Leave to cool for 15 minutes, before removing the muffins from the tin and placing them on a wire rack to cool completely.

BLUEBERRY MUFFINS

Makes: 12 muffins or 16 fairy cake-sized muffins (Vegetarian)

These are the perfect breakfast muffins, full of flavour, but not too sickly sweet. Bake them on lazy weekend mornings to enjoy while still warm, or whip up a batch at night so that they're ready for a speedy weekday breakfast.

250g plain flour

½ tsp bicarbonate of soda

1 tbsp baking powder

Pinch of salt

125g light brown soft sugar

125g butter, melted

100ml milk

2 medium eggs, beaten

200g fresh blueberries

Tip: This is a great way to use up any blueberries that have gone squidgy.

* Preheat the oven to 200°C Fan/Gas Mark 7. Line your muffin tray with the appropriately sized cake cases.

* Sift the flour, bicarbonate of soda, baking powder and salt through a sieve into a large mixing bowl. Add the sugar and stir in.

* Pour in the melted butter, milk, beaten eggs and blueberries and stir gently until just combined. Try not to mix too much or the muffins will turn out heavy and dense.

* Divide the mixture evenly among the cake cases and bake for 16–20 minutes for muffins and 12–16 minutes for fairy cakes until well risen and golden brown.

* Leave the muffins to cool in the tins for at least 20 minutes after removing from the oven. Then transfer them in their cases to a wire rack to cool fully.

BANANA MUFFINS

Makes: 12 muffins or 16 fairy cake-sized muffins (Vegetarian)

A great way to use up ripe bananas, these lovely moist muffins are a brilliant energy boost to kick off the day.

290ml milk

1 tsp lemon juice

285g self-raising flour

½ tsp bicarbonate of soda

½ tsp baking powder

Pinch of salt

190g caster sugar

100g butter, melted

1 large egg, beaten

2 large ripe bananas, mashed

* Preheat the oven to 190°C Fan/Gas Mark 6. Line your muffin tray with the appropriately sized cake cases.

* Measure out the milk into a measuring jug. Add the lemon juice, stir and set aside.

* Sift the flour, bicarbonate of soda, baking powder and salt through a sieve into a large mixing bowl. Add the sugar and stir in.

* Pour in the milk mixture, add the melted butter, beaten egg and mashed banana. Stir together gently until just combined. Try not to mix too much or the muffins will turn out heavy and dense.

* Divide the batter evenly among the cake cases and bake for 25–30 minutes for muffins and 20–25 minutes for fairy cakes until well risen and golden brown.

* Leave the muffins to cool in the tins for at least 20 minutes after removing from the oven. Then transfer them in their cases to a wire rack to cool fully.

PORRIDGE

Makes: 1 small portion (double up if you're extra-hungry) (Vegetarian)

One of the most nutritious breakfast options, porridge is also one of the cheapest. Even better, oats really fill you up and help prevent your stomach rumbling mid-lecture!

25g porridge oats
4 tbsp milk
4 tbsp water

* Place the oats, milk and water in a saucepan over a medium heat.

* Stir regularly for around 3 minutes until the oats have absorbed much of the liquid.

* Pour the porridge into a bowl and add your choice of topping. You may wish to add another tablespoon of milk to thin your porridge and cool it down if you're in a rush.

PORRIDGE TOPPINGS:

BANANA AND RASPBERRY

Serves: 1 (Vegetarian)

½–1 banana
Handful of fresh or defrosted frozen raspberries
Sugar or syrup, if desired

* Slice your banana thinly onto the hot porridge in your bowl.

* Add some raspberries, and sugar or syrup if you have a sweet tooth.

* Stir together gently and eat immediately.

CINNAMON SUGAR

Serves: 1 (Vegetarian)

1 tbsp sugar (ideally brown)
½ tsp ground cinnamon

* Simply place your hot porridge in a bowl and sprinkle the sugar and cinnamon over the top.

* Stir well and tuck in.

APPLE AND DATE

Serves: 1 (Vegetarian)

1 eating apple, peeled, cored and cut into 1cm chunks

5 dates, chopped into 1cm pieces

Sugar or syrup, if desired

* Add the apple and date pieces to the hot porridge in your bowl, and stir in.

* If you like your porridge sweeter, add a teaspoon of sugar or syrup and stir this in too.

* Eat immediately.

TOASTED NUTS AND HONEY

Serves: 1 (Vegetarian)

Handful of natural nuts of your choice

1–2 tsp honey

* Place the nuts into a dry frying pan on a medium heat.

* Allow the nuts to toast gently – you will start to smell them toasting. Take care not to let them burn. This should take around 2 minutes.

* When the nuts are toasted, transfer them to a chopping board and chop them up into small pieces using a sharp knife.

* Sprinkle the toasted nuts over your cooked porridge, and add honey to taste.

CHOCOLATE AND PECAN NUT

Serves: 1 (Vegetarian)

3–4 squares of chocolate (dark or milk as you like)

5 pecan nuts

* Chop your chocolate and pecan nuts up into small pieces.

* Sprinkle the chopped chocolate and nuts onto your hot porridge and stir through. The chocolate will quickly melt into the porridge.

* Eat immediately.

SWEETS

FIVE-MINUTE CAKE IN A MUG

Serves: 1 (Vegetarian)

For times when you're craving something sweet, but have nothing in the cupboard and can't be bothered to go to the shops, this your answer – instant chocolate cake! You can't go wrong with this super-quick recipe, but you do need a microwave for it.

1 medium egg
3 tbsp sunflower oil
3 tbsp milk
1 tsp vanilla extract
5 tbsp self-raising flour
1 tbsp cocoa powder
4½ tbsp caster sugar

* Crack the egg into a large mug and whisk really well.

* Pour the oil, milk and vanilla extract into the mug. Whisk together vigorously using a fork.

* Sift the flour and cocoa powder through a sieve into a bowl, and spoon into the mug. Add the sugar, and whisk all the ingredients together vigorously for a good minute until all the flour is incorporated. Be careful to whisk in all the flour from around the bottom of the mug. The mixture should be smooth and thick.

* Place the mug in the microwave (make sure you remove the fork!)

* Set the microwave to high and cook the cake for 90 seconds. With a powerful microwave it should be cooked after this time. If not, add another 20 seconds and check again. Touch it gently with your finger to check it. When cooked, the cake will be well risen, to the top of the mug or above, and look like a glossy sponge. It springs back when pressed.

* The cake will sink as it comes out of the microwave (take care when removing as the mug will be hot), but should only sink 1–2cm below the rim of the mug. When cool enough, eat from the mug with a spoon.

CHOCOLATE MOUSSE

Serves: 4 (Vegetarian)

Chocolate mousse is deceptively simple to make but perfect to feed to friends as it tastes so luxurious. Even better, it needs to be made in advance, leaving you free to socialise instead of stuck in the kitchen.

135g chocolate (a mix of milk and dark 70% cocoa works well)

4 large eggs

* Melt the chocolate. You can do this in a non-metallic bowl in the microwave (make sure you check it every 20 seconds so that it does not burn) or in a heatproof bowl over a small saucepan of simmering water. Stir regularly and, once melted, set aside to cool.

* Separate the eggs by placing the egg whites into one large (very clean) bowl and the egg yolks into a second bowl. Set the yolks aside.

* Whisk the egg whites vigorously until they are stiff and firm. If you have an electric whisk, it is helpful to use here.

* Add the egg yolks, one at a time, to the cooled chocolate, beating well after each addition.

* Next, add a tablespoon of the egg whites and gently fold in with a metal spoon. Do not whisk or beat as this will knock all the air out of the mousse.

* Carefully add the rest of the egg whites, a tablespoon at a time, and gently fold in to incorporate.

* Pour the mousse into a big dish or into individual glasses or cups, cover with cling film and leave to chill in the fridge for at least 3 hours before serving.

QUICK TIRAMISU

Serves: 4–6 (Vegetarian)

This creamy, coffee-flavoured treat is super-simple to put together.
If possible, make it a day in advance and leave to chill in the fridge so
the flavours can intensify. If you already have a bottle of Tia Maria
this is a great use for it, else pick up a small one and save the rest for
cocktails (or pop a sneaky shot into a coffee!).

200g sponge fingers
300ml strong coffee, cooled
120ml Tia Maria
400g ready-made custard
250g mascarpone
150ml double cream
2 tbsp cocoa powder, to dust

* Lay the sponge fingers out in a large bowl or serving dish.
  It needs to be about 1.5 litres in capacity.

* In a jug, mix the coffee and Tia Maria together and pour over
  the sponge fingers, so that they are well covered in the liquid.

* Put the custard and mascarpone in a bowl and beat together
  well. Pour evenly over the sponge fingers.

* Whisk the double cream until it is thickly whipped and stiff,
  and spoon over the custard and mascarpone layer.

* Cover with cling film and chill in the fridge for as long as you
  can before serving – overnight is ideal.

* Dust with cocoa powder and serve.

BANOFFEE PIE

Serves: 6–8 (Vegetarian)

One of the all-time most popular desserts, this gooey treat is even easier to make than you might think, as it involves absolutely no cooking and is just a simple assembly job.

250g digestive biscuits

100g butter, melted, plus extra for greasing

400g can of canned caramel

3 bananas

300ml double cream, whipped

1 tbsp cocoa powder, to dust

* Start by making the base. Lightly grease a 20cm springform cake tin and set aside.

* Place the biscuits in a plastic food bag and bash using a rolling pin or similar implement until the biscuits resemble dust. Be careful not to use anything sharp that might pierce the bag.

* Empty the biscuit crumbs into a mixing bowl and stir in the melted butter. Tip this mixture into your prepared tin and press down evenly to cover the base of the tin. Build the mixture up the sides to about 3cm high to form a biscuit shell to encase the filling. Chill in the fridge for 2 hours.

* When the base has been chilled, pour the caramel onto the biscuit base. Spread in an even layer over the bottom of the base.

* Slice the bananas and lay them out on top of the caramel.

* Finally, place the whipped cream on top of the bananas and spread evenly. Chill the pie in the fridge for an hour or two before removing from the tin, dusting lightly with cocoa powder and serving.

POACHED PEARS WITH LEFTOVER RED WINE

Serves: 4 (Vegetarian)

What to do with leftover red wine? These poached pears are quick and straightforward to prepare, full of flavour and look very impressive. Make them a day before you want them and they'll taste even better. If you or your friends are vegetarian, do check the wine you use here is suitable.

4 large ripe pears
600ml red wine
1 cinnamon stick
Grated zest of 1 orange
Grated zest of 1 unwaxed lemon
200g caster sugar
1 tsp vanilla extract
Cream or ice cream, to serve

* Peel the pears, making sure you leave the stalk on. It looks prettier if you peel them lengthways.

* Place the peeled pears into a saucepan. Add the remaining ingredients.

* Put the saucepan on a gentle heat and allow the pears to gently bubble away in the wine for 30 minutes.

* Remove the pears from the sauce and set aside on a plate.

* Turn up the heat and allow the wine sauce to bubble away for a further 15 minutes. Keep stirring regularly until the sauce has reduced down and is thick and syrupy.

* Serve the pears and thickened red wine sauce either hot or cold, with cream or ice cream on the side.

SUMMER BERRY FOOL

Serves: 2 (Vegetarian)

A naughty but light pudding that tastes of summer. Use any berries you like – strawberries and raspberries work particularly well. It's a great way to use up any berries that are going soft and squidgy. Nice served with a shortbread biscuit.

100g fresh summer berries
100ml double cream
1 tbsp icing sugar

* Wash and dry the berries thoroughly using kitchen towel. They need to be completely dry when you start to make this.

* In a mixing bowl, whisk the cream until it is thickly whipped.

* Place the berries in a large bowl. Sift the icing sugar through a sieve over the berries and lightly mash them until they are broken up slightly.

* Place the berries into the cream gently. Avoid adding any juice from the berries – dry them again if necessary.

* Gently stir the fruit into the cream until evenly distributed but not so vigorously that you end up bashing all the air out of the cream.

* If the fool is a bit stiff, you can add a little fruit juice to thin it slightly.

* Serve and enjoy immediately.

APPLE GALETTES

Makes: 6–8, depending on cutter size (Vegetarian)

These gorgeous-looking little pastries give the impression you've taken lots of time and effort making them but are in fact very simple to put together. They taste wonderful served warm with vanilla ice cream or whipped cream.

375g packet of ready-rolled puff pastry

2 tbsp apricot jam

3–4 eating apples

2 tbsp ground almonds

40g caster sugar

1 tsp ground cinnamon

* Preheat the oven to 180°C Fan/Gas Mark 6.

* Line a large baking sheet with a sheet of non-stick baking paper and set aside.

* Unroll the pastry onto a floured work surface. Cut the pastry into discs using a cookie cutter or drinking glass, approximately 9cm in diameter, or into rectangles, whatever is easier. Place the pastry shapes onto the baking sheet.

* Heat the apricot jam gently in a small saucepan until it becomes runny.

* Meanwhile, peel the apples and cut out the cores. Cut lengthways into thin slices.

* Brush the runny apricot jam over each piece of pastry. Sprinkle the ground almonds evenly over the top of the jam.

* Lay the slices of apple over each pastry base, ensuring the slices are overlapping.

* Brush each galette with more apricot jam to cover the apples and the pastry.

* Mix the caster sugar and cinnamon together in a small bowl. Sprinkle evenly over each galette.

* Bake the galettes in the oven for 20–25 minutes until the pastry is golden brown and the apples are tender. Serve hot or cold.

BAKED LEMON PUDDING

Serves: 4 (Vegetarian)

This fuss-free sponge pudding is packed full of zesty deliciousness and is great served warm with ice cream.

75g butter, softened,
plus extra for greasing

275g caster sugar

Grated zest of 1 lemon

2 medium eggs, beaten

90ml lemon juice

300ml milk

60g self-raising flour

1 tsp baking powder

* Preheat the oven to 180°C Fan/Gas Mark 6.

* Grease a 1 litre-capacity ovenproof baking dish with butter and set aside.

* In a mixing bowl beat together the butter, sugar and lemon zest, using a wooden spoon or electric mixer, until pale and fluffy.

* Add the beaten eggs and mix together well, followed by the lemon juice and milk.

* Sift the flour and baking powder through a sieve into the bowl and stir together to form a runny batter.

* Pour the mixture into the prepared dish and bake for 40–50 minutes until sponge-like on top and crisp around the edges. Serve hot or cold.

CHOCOLATE NUT COOKIES

Makes: 8–10 cookies (Vegetarian)

Crisp at the edges and soft in the middle, these cookies are extremely hard to resist! They keep well in an airtight box, if they haven't already been gobbled up by greedy housemates, that is!

100g butter, softened

100g light brown soft sugar

65g demerara sugar

1 large egg, beaten

1 tsp vanilla extract

165g plain flour

35g cocoa powder

½ tsp baking powder

½ tsp bicarbonate of soda

Generous pinch of salt

50g chocolate chips or chocolate chunks

50g nuts of your choice (pecans and walnuts are very good here)

* Preheat the oven to 170°C Fan/Gas Mark 5.

* Line two large baking sheets with non-stick baking paper.

* In a large mixing bowl, beat together the butter and both types of sugar, using a wooden spoon or electric mixer, until pale and fluffy.

* Combine the beaten egg and vanilla extract, then add them to the mixture gradually, mixing well after each addition.

* Sift the flour, cocoa powder, baking powder, bicarbonate of soda and salt through a sieve into the bowl, and mix well until thoroughly combined.

* Add the chocolate and nuts and mix well.

* Pinch off golf ball-sized pieces of mixture. Roll into balls and place on the prepared baking sheets, well spaced apart.

* Dust the base of a flat-bottomed drinking glass with flour and use it to press down on each cookie to flatten.

* Bake the cookies for 8–10 minutes until firm to the touch.

* Allow the cookies to cool on the baking sheets for 10 minutes before transferring to a wire rack to cool fully.

S'MORES

Serves: 1

A s'more is a traditional American campfire treat of chocolate and marshmallow melted between two biscuits. They're a very easy treat to put together in a flash when you fancy something sweet.

2 digestive biscuits

2 squares of milk chocolate

2 marshmallows

* Preheat the grill to a medium temperature.

* Lay out the biscuits on a small piece of foil.

* Place one square of chocolate and one marshmallow on each biscuit.

* Now, grill the biscuits for approximately 2 minutes, until the chocolate is melted and the marshmallow is browned.

* Sandwich the two biscuits together and enjoy immediately.

CHOCOLATE, BANANA AND COOKIE ICE CREAM

Serves: 6 (Vegetarian)

Why splash the cash on a tub of premium ice cream when it's so easy to make your own? This recipe doesn't even require an ice cream machine – just an electric whisk. Flavourwise, it doesn't get better than this indulgent combo. Keep in the freezer for when you fancy a treat.

300ml double cream

60g caster sugar

3 ripe bananas, mashed

50g chocolate chips

50g cookies, of your choice, chopped into 1–2cm chunks

1 tbsp lemon juice

* Place the cream into a large mixing bowl and whisk until thickly whipped. Use an electric whisk if you have one.

* Beat the caster sugar and mashed banana into the cream.

* Add the chocolate chips, cookie chunks (making sure you discard any crumbs) and lemon juice. Gently fold into the mixture.

* Pour into a plastic tub, seal and freeze. After 2 hours, remove from the freezer and beat well with a wooden spoon. Return to the freezer and repeat after another 2 hours.

* Return the ice cream to the freezer. It is now ready to eat whenever you want it.

HOMEMADE MERINGUE NESTS

Makes: 4 nests (Vegetarian)

Whisking up egg whites may sound scary, but home-made meringues are actually super-easy to make and have a gorgeous chewy texture. Use an electric hand whisk if you can – it makes life much easier!

3 large egg whites
Pinch of salt
115g caster sugar

* Preheat the oven to 140°C Fan/Gas Mark 3. Line a large baking sheet with non-stick baking paper.

* Ensure your mixing bowl (not plastic) and whisk are spotlessly clean and dry before you start. (This is important because any dust or grease will prevent the egg whites from whipping up.)

* Place the egg whites and pinch of salt in the mixing bowl. Whisk until the egg whites become white and foamy. Add the sugar a tablespoon at a time, whisking well after addition. Continue to whisk until the meringue is thick, sticky and glossy. It should be so firm it stays in place when the bowl is turned upside down.

* Spoon the meringue out onto the paper in mounds, about 2 tablespoons of meringue for each, and form into a round shape with the back of a spoon.

* Bake the meringues in the oven for 25 minutes, then turn off the oven and leave to cool completely for several hours or overnight. Avoid opening the oven door during this time.

* The cooked meringues will keep for several weeks in an airtight container.

BERRY AND CREAM MERINGUES

Serves: 4 (Vegetarian)

Make a scrumptious pudding in a matter of minutes using the meringue nests above or shop-bought ones if you want to cheat.

4 meringue nests
50ml double cream, whipped
100g berries (use whichever fresh berries take your fancy)
1 tbsp icing sugar, to dust

* Set the meringue nests out on plates.

* Divide the whipped cream among the meringue nests. Top with berries and sift icing sugar through a sieve to dust.

* Serve immediately as the meringue will go soft if kept for long.

VANILLA ICE CREAM WITH TEQUILA CHOCOLATE SAUCE

Serves: 4 (Vegetarian)

Pimp your ice cream with this seriously yummy Tequila-spiked chocolate sauce. (Save the rest of the bottle for Margarita cocktails, or if you don't want to buy a whole bottle see if you can borrow a shot from a generous housemate!) This is a speedy dessert for a crowd or just as good as a naughty pudding for one (reduce the quantities).

75g dark chocolate (preferably 70% cocoa solids)

3 tbsp double cream

1 tbsp tequila

Vanilla ice cream (1–2 scoops per person)

Few generous pinches of ground cinnamon, to sprinkle

* Melt the chocolate. You can do this in a non-metallic bowl in the microwave (check it every 20 seconds so that it doesn't burn) or in a heatproof bowl over a small pan of simmering water (make sure the water isn't touching the bottom of the bowl). Stir regularly. Once melted, set aside to cool.

* Stir the cream and tequila gradually into the melted chocolate.

* Place your vanilla ice cream in bowls and pour over the chocolate sauce. It is normal for the sauce to harden when poured onto the cold ice cream.

* Finish with a sprinkle of cinnamon and serve right away.

Tips: You can make this without tequila if you prefer a non-alcoholic version.

BANANA BREAD

Serves: 8 (Vegetarian)

Called 'bread' because it is less sweet and more substantial than your typical cake, this is brilliant for an energy boost at any time of the day. The fruit makes it lovely and moist – for the best outcome use really ripe bananas. Perfect with a cup of tea.

100g sultanas

150g butter

3 bananas, mashed

2 large eggs, beaten

75g caster sugar

75g light brown muscovado sugar

275g self-raising flour

½ tsp bicarbonate of soda

* Preheat the oven to 170°C Fan/Gas Mark 5.

* Grease and line a 900g loaf tin with non-stick baking paper.

* Put the sultanas into a bowl and pour over enough boiling water to cover them. Set aside.

* Melt the butter in a saucepan over a low heat or in a non-metallic bowl in the microwave.

* Mash the banana in a bowl. Add the eggs and both types of sugar and mix until well combined.

* Sift the flour and bicarbonate of soda through a sieve into the bowl and stir in.

* Drain the sultanas and stir them into the mixture.

* Pour the mixture into the prepared cake tin and bake for 1 hour until well risen and deep brown in colour, and a skewer or cocktail stick inserted into the middle of the loaf comes out clean.

* Allow to cool for 20 minutes in the tin, then remove from the tin, peel off the baking paper and place on a wire rack to cool fully.

BAILEYS CHEESECAKE

Serves: 8–10 (Vegetarian)

This luscious cheesecake is straightforward to make and doesn't even need the oven! You can use the rest of the Baileys for cocktails or a cheeky Irish coffee, or even to spike cupcakes or brownies.

For the base

12 digestive biscuits

80g butter, melted

For the topping

400g full-fat cream cheese

300ml double cream, whipped

100g icing sugar, sifted

75ml Baileys

2 tbsp cocoa powder, to dust

* Lightly grease a 20cm round springform cake tin and set aside.

* Place the biscuits in a plastic food bag and bash using a rolling pin or similar implement until the biscuits resemble dust. Be careful not to use anything sharp or it might pierce the bag.

* Empty the biscuit crumbs into a mixing bowl and stir in the melted butter. Tip this mixture into your prepared tin and flatten it down evenly to cover the base of the tin. Set aside.

* In a bowl, beat the cream cheese with a wooden spoon. Make sure the double cream is whipped stiffly, and then add it to the cream cheese with the sifted icing sugar and Baileys, and stir together gently.

* Gently spoon the cheesecake mixture into the tin over the biscuit base and make sure the top is even and smooth.

* Chill for at least 4 hours, if not overnight, before dusting with cocoa powder and cutting into slices to serve.

DOUBLE CHOCOLATE CHUNK BROWNIES

Makes: 10–14 brownies (Vegetarian)

These gooey, fudgy brownies are a real treat. They can be made in advance if you wish and taste even better a day or two after baking. Use the best-quality chocolate you can afford – it makes all the difference to the finished brownies. You can even serve them warm with ice cream for pudding.

100g dark chocolate
(preferably 70% cocoa solids)

120g butter

150g dark brown soft sugar

150g caster sugar

1 tsp vanilla extract

2 large eggs, beaten

150g plain flour

Pinch of salt

100g chocolate chunks

* Preheat the oven to 170°C Fan/Gas Mark 5.

* Line a 20cm square cake tin with non-stick baking paper. Set aside.

* Melt the chocolate and butter together. You can do this in a non-metallic bowl in the microwave (make sure you check it every 20 seconds so that it does not burn) or in a heatproof bowl over a small saucepan of simmering water.

* When the chocolate and butter are melted, mix vigorously to combine. Set aside and allow to cool for 10 minutes or so.

* Stir the two types of sugar together in a mixing bowl.

* Add the vanilla extract and beaten eggs and whisk together vigorously until well mixed.

* Pour in the cooled melted chocolate and butter and stir to combine well.

* Sift the flour and salt through a sieve into the bowl and gently stir in, followed by the chocolate chunks.

* Pour the mixture into the prepared tin and bake for 20–25 minutes until the top is nice and glossy. Be careful not to overcook or the brownies will be on the dry side.

* Allow to cool fully before cutting into slices.

BERRY AND APPLE CRUMBLE

Serves: 4 (Vegetarian)

A classic fruit crumble is one of the cheapest and simplest puds you can make and ideal for feeding a crowd, perhaps to round off a hearty Sunday lunch.

For the fruit

400g apples, peeled,
cored and sliced

400g berries (any type you like)

30g demerara sugar

For the crumble topping

100g plain flour

65g cold butter, cut into cubes

50g demerara sugar

50g oats

Ice cream, custard or cream,
to serve

* Preheat the oven to 200°C Fan/Gas Mark 7.

* Place the prepared apples and berries in the bottom of a 1.5 litre-capacity ovenproof dish. Sprinkle the demerara sugar evenly over the fruit.

* To make the crumble topping, place the flour and butter into a bowl. Rub together using the tips of your fingers until the mixture looks like breadcrumbs.

* Add the sugar and oats and stir into the mixture.

* Sprinkle the crumble topping evenly over the fruit.

* Bake for 30–40 minutes until the topping is golden and the fruit is soft.

* Serve hot or cold with ice cream, custard or cream.

Tip: You can use fresh or frozen berries. It's a good way to use up any berries that are past their prime.

INDEX

Page numbers in **bold** denote an illustration

AUTHOR'S ACKNOWLEDGEMENTS

Thank you to my fantastic agent, Clare Hulton, for seeing something in me, and for all your support, guidance and answers to my numerous questions.

Sincerest thanks to Jenny Heller at Quercus for your vision, enthusiasm and backing. It is a great pleasure and privilege to work with you. Thank you to Ione Walder for so expertly guiding me through every step and for being a complete and utter joy to work with, and thanks indeed to everyone at Quercus for all your hard work. Caroline and Clive at Harris + Wilson, Jonathan Cherry and Lincoln Jefferson, thank you for a brilliant photo shoot, and for being such fun to work with. Thanks also to A-Side studio for your great design and layout.

Many thanks are due to every single member of my testing team for going above and beyond to triple-test each recipe. I'm also lucky to have so many wonderful friends who haven't forgotten me despite how elusive I've been over the last couple of years. Thanks for sticking with me and for your constant support. Thank you to Philippa Wadsworth for all your time and advice, and to Alexandra Wilby, Judith Arkle and Claire Reid for kindly allowing me to adapt your recipes.

Thank you to all my family for your support and encouragement. Particular thanks to Claire Crook for all your help testing recipes, and to Louise Martin for being there from day one. Thank you for all those long days spent in the kitchen and for keeping me smiling amidst the chaos. Special thanks to Jean Harker for your time, generosity, wisdom and advice. Thank you to my wonderful sister, Lucy, for absolutely everything. I know I ask you for a lot of help. Thanks too, to Andy for being awesome.

I couldn't do what I do now without the never-ending support and generosity of my parents. Although I am supposed to be grown up, I really could not manage without everything you do for me, so thank you. Finally, thank you to Tony, for everything.

Quercus Editions Ltd
55 Baker Street
7th Floor, South Block
London
W1U 8EW

First published in 2013

A catalogue record of this book is available from the British Library

ISBN 978 1 78206 006 2

Publishing Director: Jenny Heller
Project Editor: Ione Walder
Produced by: Harris + Wilson
Design: A-Side Studio
Food styling: Lincoln Jefferson

Printed and bound in China

10 9 8 7 6 5 4 3 2 1